*To Amy, Emily and James for tolerating
my endless distraction.*

*To Dan and the team at Santy for inspiring
my endless distraction.*

UNDER THINK IT

A MARKETING STRATEGY GUIDEBOOK FOR EVERYONE

ADAM PIERNO

CHAPTERS

Introduction

~ *or* ~

1. WHY THIS BOOK?

Every startup has its founder's story, the myth of its creation. And we are obsessed with them. This book is the result of a string of events which are entirely un-mythic. Today I lead the strategy team at Santy, a 50-person advertising agency based in Scottsdale. But earlier in my career I was an Art Director and eventually a Creative Director. My career began at big firms in Boston and New York, so access to strategy was simple.

I was at Hill, Holliday when account planning was introduced in the agency. In fact, at the announcement of the new discipline, one of the copywriters asked "Isn't a planner just another person who can kill my work?" As it turns out, the initial group of planners proved to be much more valuable than that. We had no shortage of information about our clients from that team. Moving to JWT, there were even more tools and information sources available. A bigger and more experienced group of planners and researchers. Any question I had, there was a team of smart people to answer it for me.

But moving to smaller agencies outside these big metro markets, this information was harder to come by. As a Creative Director, I partnered with the account and media directors to fill the role of account planning as a team at Santy. This was an extremely lucky break for my career and, though I didn't know it at the time, the beginnings of this book. Not having a full research or strategy team taught me to be resourceful and find the information I wanted. Even better, it taught me how to filter and understand what information I should seek out.

When we launched a strategy team at Santy, there were no processes in place. I moved over from a career as a creative and got the opportunity to figure it out in real time. This was both a blessing and a curse. Three years in, and the strategy team has become a hub of the agency - integral to client business and (hopefully) useful to the account and creative teams. The team began to grow and I was asked to begin training agency staffers and new strategy team members.

It seemed simple enough. But as I began creating the training materials, I realized I had never been given any. No formal training. Just what I've absorbed from co-workers, articles and places like Twitter. I didn't know where to start. So I treated the training syllabus like a strategy assignment.

STEP 1? GOOGLE IT.

Articles began piling up in my bookmarks, but I couldn't find what I was looking for: A single, comprehensive course on marketing strategy. I reached out to friends and colleagues and their answer - "If you find something please send it my way." It seems strategists and planners of all levels across the country were also looking for this single course.

I couldn't find it, so I started writing down what we do every day. I started training the Santy team with the curriculum and I realized something. If our 50-person agency needed the training, other agencies probably did too.

I began formalizing the curriculum and offering trainings to agencies and brands looking for some support.

Here's why this approach is different. I came from the creative world. I have seen some great briefs and I have seen some absolutely terrible briefs. I have seen awful focus groups kill solid work like an angry mob and I have worked with skilled moderators who coaxed the right information to improve work that needed a push. At Santy, we've built a strategy team focused on getting it right for the work and the clients more than we get it wrong. We're not perfect, but we're looking at a broader context than just strategy and planning as an academic enterprise.

The training I created and this book are tools to help people become more informed about their client's business and more useful to them. As agency or marketers, we come to the table and expect to be treated as partners with our clients, but most times we don't behave very much like partners. They hear the ideas we pitch as distraction or extra work.

If we want to be treated as partners we have to bring them the business rationale behind our ideas. We have to make the business case for the idea they will be asked to pay for before they ask for one. We have to prove we know what the hell we're talking about. They want to know what will this cost. What will it return? How it can be simpler? But they also need to know why we've recommended one path over another.

This book is not meant to be an encyclopedia of strategy, or the single source for all strategy thinking for your entire career. It is meant to be picked up whenever you or someone on your team is starting a new project and looking for reinforcement or reminding of some of the fundamentals of what we do. Read it cover to cover, dog ear the pages you find useful, come back to them when you need to. When I'm stealing from someone throughout the book, I'll mention them by name. There's a bibliography at the back of the book for your use. I'm hoping this book is part of a foundation of learning about strategy.

WHO IS THIS BOOK FOR?

We designed this training for our strategy team first. But a funny thing happened. People across the agency asked to be trained. Art directors, account executives, paid search specialists, content managers. We began to see common themes and forget the idea that this was just for planners and strategists. Forget about the role in the organization. We did. Think instead about what you hope to learn or why.

THE MOTIVATED.

Staff who want to advance in their career by doing and selling better work. These people want the foundation in strategy to help get to better ideas quickly and present them in a way that clients can buy in to. They see this training as a platform to help them improve and move forward.

THE CURIOUS.

Why do people do what they do? How did the client get to this conclusion? Is this brief really the best it could be? These people always have questions about marketing, audiences and the way the world works. They see the curriculum as a way to answer some of their questions and guide others.

THE NEWCOMERS.

Advertising agencies are typically awful places for training. Especially smaller agencies. It's not because people aren't interested in training new staff and it's not because new staff doesn't want to be trained. If you've spent an hour in any agency, you already know it's because every minute of every employee is put to use for clients. The best and brightest in the agency who would make the best teachers and mentors are typically the most demanded by clients and conferences.

Like any other type of communication, this book is useless unless it's made relevant to the reader. Who is this book for? As part of the curriculum I created, I included a module on personas (which I will discuss in detail in Chapter 8). You have probably already written some for client projects. I have created some custom personas based on who will be interested in the training behind this book.

Three personas make up the agency staff that will benefit the most from the training. Here are adapted versions of those people.

KAT (AGENCY PLANNER)
28, Female, College Graduate, Dallas, TX
Kat is in her second job as a planner. She wants to grow in her career, but doesn't know where to turn for comprehensive training. She knows there is a lot to learn, but isn't even sure what all of it is. She uses Skillshare and chats on the OpenStrategy Slack channel. She gets excited by ideas as she gets exposed to them. There are a lot of individual resources but Kat is hoping to string some together to have context.

MIKE (STRATEGY DIRECTOR)
44, Male, College Graduate, Philadelphia, PA
Mike wants to help train the only planner on his staff, and is looking for a way to train some account executives to

participate more in writing briefs and selling projects involving research. He spends some time mentoring one-on-one and recommends books to expose his team to ideas but has trouble closing the loop with them. He wants to pitch bigger brands and is concerned he doesn't have the resources to go toe-to-toe with agencies in bigger markets.

JAMES (PRINCIPAL)
60, Male, College Graduate, Portland, OR
James wants the agency to grow - quickly. He's focused on networking with prospects and is constantly hearing and reading that brands don't think agencies are strategically on pace. He doesn't want the agency to be out-of-date and sees an opportunity to grow organically with just a little strategic firepower. When he sends his staff to conferences they come back with inspiration that quickly fades.

As you can see, the experience and professional context of these three personas differs widely. James won't likely be the best recipient of this book, if you are wondering whom to pass it on to next.

On the other hand, some agency principals may benefit from the ideas, which may be a refresher or be presented in a different way. Not everyone who has a stake in an agency or manages marketing thinkers have been trained themselves! I hope the "Jameses" of the world would be inspired to provide training for their staff. This can only help the organization improve and become more trusted advisors for brands.

Mike may not need this book because he has been lucky enough to have received some training and practices his craft every day. Or, in reading the concepts shared in the following chapters, he may be able to borrow (or flat-out steal, that's what I did) the core concepts to train his own team. I am thrilled at this prospect. To be fair, the content in the book is mostly a series of reminders for Mike. Reminders aren't bad, and I've found having a toolkit I can refer back to is valuable to keep me grounded as I begin or revisit projects. Mike should want his team to have access to this information. And as the persona illustrates, he likely doesn't have time.

Kat wants the information in this book or something like it. In many agencies and businesses, Kat is responsible for identifying her own training opportunities, though that responsibility is rarely discussed. Young people are required to research conferences and classes and muster the courage to ask for the funds to attend, or else to pay out of pocket. Books like this one and those in the bibliography are simple ways to offer career enrichment.

2. WHY SO SERIOUS?

So much of the content available about marketing strategy is unduly serious. Lots of big words, very few laughs. Why? It's weird because we treat strategy as a series of puzzles to be solved by curious people who enjoy doing puzzles. Of course it's fun.

Like any puzzle, strategy's often stone-faced tone can also be solved. There are reasons for the jargon. Some of the concepts that drive strategy come from academic or other professional fields like consulting. Fifty-cent words tend to fly. Once those words make it to agencies or marketers, we hold on to the terms tightly. Here's why.

WE ARE TERRIFIED WE ARE GOING TO BE REVEALED AS FRAUDS.

Going right back to the point about academic concepts driving jargon, the term Impostor Syndrome was presented by clinical psychologists Pauline R. Clance and Suzanne A. Imes in the late 1970s. According to their research, many people - even high performers - lack the confidence that they meet the standards or baseline metrics of their profession or activity. They later unsuccessfully tried to rename it 'Impostor Experience.'

People lacking that confidence often use big words as a defense mechanism.

WE WANT TO DIFFERENTIATE FROM OUR COMPETITION.

Agencies are guilty of this very, very often. How many agency decks have you seen (or helped write!) in which the same ideas or processes are given a branded title or referred to as proprietary? My guess is: a lot. When a new concept is learned from an academic publication or at a conference, agencies tend to try to turn it into a product that can be sold to brands. The first few will lift the academic ~~nomenclature~~ name, followed by the next few who will give it a new even 'smarter' sounding name.

WE WANT TO SOUND SMART.
We can't all be Faris Yakob or Tom Goodwin. They are
exceptionally smart people who have the benefit of
sounding smart pretty naturally. They've earned a following
by sharing big ideas they've learned or experienced. (The
accents don't hurt, either.) Especially for strategy staff, we
believe we must imply intelligence to have influence. We
use big words to make ourselves distinctively brilliant. See?
I could have just said 'make ourselves sound smart' but I
was trying to make you think that I'm smart so you'd
continue reading.

There's nothing wrong with any of the above. Agencies
should try to differentiate. Smart people should not be
afraid to be viewed as such. Insecurity can present itself in a
lot of ways, big words are one of the better byproducts.

Here's the problem. In order for you to have the influence
you want to have - to be effective in sharing your ideas - the
audience has to understand you. Big words might separate
you from the other people in the room, but they will also
create a division between the ideas and their minds. The
harder they have to work to understand, the harder they
will have to work to explain it to their boss. That makes it
harder to buy from you, or in some cases - to trust you.

This doesn't mean things have to be 'dumbed down.' They
shouldn't. They just need to be presented clearly. The best
way to be clear is to use a common vocabulary (and visuals).
Don't read what isn't written here. By common vocabulary I
mean the words everyone in the room uses. There are times

when industry jargon is the common vocabulary. In that case, to make your point, use the client's jargon if it will make it simpler to understand and to sell.

When bringing a new strategic concept to a client, or to others in the agency, find better words than the academic publication used. Put the concept into a new context that clarifies it for the creative team, the media team or the client. Speak their language, but do it smartly.

This is a critical point. You will note throughout the book the use of strikethrough text on ~~superfluously~~ big words. This is the editor's way of reiterating the point - simpler words make things more clear.

There is something else at play. When we choose complicated words over simpler ones, we make a choice. Though some will try to follow along, others will come to another conclusion: that we are doing it ~~deliberately~~ purposefully to make our ideas hard to understand. This not only wrecks the desired effect of our work, but also impacts our credibility. When people decide you are *trying* to confuse them, you've lost their trust. This applies to clients who are ever-suspicious of agency sales tactics as well as creatives or agency staff who honestly don't know what strategists and planners do all day.

Even the word 'strategy' is broad and confusing. No one is really saying the same thing when they use the word. It can touch every part of a business or be extremely specific. Are planners strategists? Depends on who you ask. There's a video that I find a bit embarrassing which asks very, very smart planners and strategists the difference between the two titles. Honestly, we know there is a difference but that doesn't matter if we're the only ones. So let's start defining things. For the purposes of this book, we will agree on a definition of strategy. An extremely simple one.

STRATEGY: USING INFORMATION TO
GUIDE FUTURE DECISIONS.

Who on an agency or marketing team should understand strategy based on that definition? I hope everyone. Clarity is one of the main principles of great strategy. The tendency is to keep people out, to use big words to make it hard to participate or to understand.

Avoid this pitfall at all costs. Strategy can be fun. Most of the time, we are not saving lives. Most advertising campaigns are designed to come up with engaging ways to sell something semi-trivial. Try to remember that. Even though we take our responsibilities seriously, we won't earn Nobel prizes for our work. Our language can reflect that.

Most of us in this business are the curious ones who like solving problems and figuring out puzzles. Don't be afraid to share the joy and enthusiasm you feel by making it ~~accessible~~ easy to follow.

That's part of the reason for this book. My intent is to take the tools and techniques that work and hand them off. I did not invent these techniques, and I have no reason to keep them secret. To be honest, just knowing they exist doesn't give anyone an advantage which is why I'm so eager to share them. The trick is knowing when to use each tool and how to use them together. Or when to do something totally different and try something new.

The more people in the organization who understand the concepts and the tools of strategy, the better the thinking can be done for the brand - and the better chance to create and sell great, effective ideas.

3. WHAT DOESN'T WORK?

On average, advertising is getting less and less effective. There will always be ideas and executions that break through, but it sure seems harder to do it. We want to bring effective ideas to our clients, and we want clients to execute those ideas. Strategy is how. Strategy allows us to find the insight that will connect with consumers in a connections plan or a TV spot. And strategy is the way we will

demonstrate to the client that we understand their business enough to have the right to bring this idea forward.
Before I start with the fundamentals of marketing strategy, let's rule out some basics. Let's start with the things that kill good thinking before it starts.

LOCKING IN

If you were nodding your head in the last chapter when I mentioned the way agencies try to trademark every basic process, you'll love this. What doesn't work when it comes to strategy today? One thing.

No, not one thing as in - just one thing that doesn't work. I mean, strategy is not a single replicable process. I truly wish it were. Every project is custom. Every strategic approach is unique. Even projects for the same brand, with the same target audience done by the same staff at the same agency may vary wildly in approach.

What?! You gasp? There's no process? No methodology?!? OK, so maybe you don't use the wild punctuation. You're not wrong to challenge here. There needs to be some process. The process might even be something resembling 'proprietary' your own

There isn't a single proprietary methodology that works for every assignment. In my experience, no two assignments are alike. And anybody that only has one skill or methodology tries to convert every problem to something they can use that skill on. Abraham Maslow's saying 'when you only have a hammer, everything looks like a nail' comes to mind. The challenging part of strategy isn't necessarily finding the answers, but finding the questions. Spending time to understand what problem exists behind the visible problem you were asked to solve is the job. Assuming everything can be done one way limits the potential for solutions.

This is an oversimplification. There is a methodology, but it's not a strategic one. It's not a framework. Answering these questions leads me to the list of questions that have to be asked and answered. If I were to boil down the job of strategy, I boil it down to the three questions I have scrawled on a sticky note on my desk.

1. WHAT IS THE REAL PROBLEM WE ARE TRYING TO SOLVE?

2. WHAT DOES SUCCESS LOOK LIKE?

3. WHAT ARE THE CONSTRAINTS?

Don't miss the point. As a strategist, you are an engineer. The work you do fits into a more complex system. One of the problems we see when we talk about strategy as a discipline is that a brilliant strategy is meaningless unless it inspires others to take brilliant actions. They don't give Jay Chiat Awards to terrible work that had the slickest brief informed by the tightest research findings. If your work doesn't compel the creative team to put in extra time to make the work amazing - and guide them to create something that touches the end user - you've missed.

What doesn't work? Academic strategy. Powerpoint strategy. Nothing you do is valuable unless you are able to influence the other people in the chain. Compelling people to act (exceptionally) is half the job. If you write a great brief and the work is mediocre, then you have failed. If your great brief inspires great work and you haven't convinced the client to act, you have failed.

With the rah rah for empowering strategy to psych up the rest of the agency out of the way, let me just say it:

The best strategic thought doesn't have to come from you.

If something you found or said sparked a genius thought, amen. If your agency is anything like Santy, it is full of really smart people. They are bound to have great insights and thoughts. You have not failed if someone else comes up with a great insight or strategy line. If it is true and right for the work, then your job is to support that insight with every tool that you have.

Now that we've established that the best idea can come from anywhere; resist the assumption that whoever did the work before you was stupid. This phenomenon is known as 'last man in.' If you've ever had someone service your car, you have witnessed this behavior. The technician leans over the engine, shakes his head and says "Wow. Whoever worked on this last was a real amateur." Really? It came from the factory and no one has touched it since except for oil changes. 180,000 miles ago.

There are really smart people in our field. Assume a person smarter than you worked on this before you. Assume they had good reasons for what they did. Assume they had good intentions. Assume it was presented to a very capable CMO, CEO and board. Assume it was working very well at some point. If it's not clear, find someone to ask or do your research. Just don't assume the person before you was an amateur, because you can guarantee they were not. Bad things happen when you're the smartest person in the room. Worse things happen when you think you are the smartest, but aren't.

One final thing that doesn't work. The data never, ever speaks for itself. In fact, if left on its own as presented in a series of charts on Powerpoint slides, the data acts more like a "Choose Your Own Adventure" book. People may see what they want to see as a condition of confirmation bias. That goes double for strategy staff. Having the skill to gather the data is fantastic, but that's just the beginning of the work. Copy/Pasting doesn't get the job done.

Your job as the strategist is to tell the story that leads to a clear conclusion. That doesn't mean carving the data to suit your story, it means finding the truth in the information you've collected and presenting it convincingly. Make it undeniable. Have a point of view and don't be shy about sharing it. Know what the point of view is and write the story to support it.

Now that I've laid out some ground rules, let's get to work.

4. MARKETING FOR STRATEGISTS

Curiously, many people find their way to agencies or in-house marketing departments at major brands without being educated or trained in the basics of marketing. And inside agencies, even more curiously, there is no additional training in marketing beyond the on the job variety. Which is a wonderful way to ensure that you will always be at least one step behind the MBAs. It's like being asked to bring a knife to a gunfight. Every. Single. Day.

It's up to you how long you want to be underprepared for these encounters. As I've researched training practices there is definitely an opportunity for companies to better teach their staff. But there also is a responsibility for individuals to learn and to drive training. At Santy, I refer to moments when a client or partner reveals information or thinking we weren't prepared for as 'getting pantsed.' There is no less pleasant feeling. Consider education a belt.

Before you move forward in this chapter, be warned. There are better books on marketing. Much better. But some of what I teach is necessary as a foundation for the the tools we use every day. This won't be a regurgitation of Marketing 101 or a glossary because I don't believe that most of these concepts apply to agencies. We are usually brought in after the actual "marketing" has been done.

Start with the marketing mix - the Four Ps which was developed in the late 1950s. Of the four, three of them - Product, Price and Place - are assigned to us 99% of the time. The agency gets to skin the last P, Promotion. This is flawed. Separating promotion from the other parts is an outmoded old thought. This is especially true with digital products, which may actually only have 2 Ps. Product, Place and Promotion may all be the same thing (ie., Squarespace).

Agencies have become much more involved in Place. There are tons of great examples of experiential campaigns and executions that help re-contextualize the Product or brand for consumers. For example, 360i helped Nestle's Lean Cuisine reframe the promise of the product by executing an experiential campaign in public spaces like New York's Grand Central Station. They invited women to define how they would like to be measured instead of weight - choosing attributes and descriptions of their accomplishments instead of pounds. An artist helped bring each to life by painting a scale which the women were invited to hand in an exhibit showcasing all of the scales. Women used phrases like "Back in College at 55" or "Caring for over 200 homeless children per day" to show that lives are more than just one metric on the scale.

The most effective client/agency relationships allow for collaboration across the spectrum of the marketing mix.

When Crispin Porter + Bogusky found research that showed consumers were eating even more on the go than was understood in 2004, they created a product - not an ad - for Burger King: Chicken Fries. The packaging is designed to fit in a car's cupholder. The product was an initial hit, and when the brand pulled Chicken Fries off the menu, fans begged for their return via reddit and other online forums. They've been on the menu ever since.

Takeaway: If you are going to make an impact on your client's business, you need to be thinking about the entire business and not waiting for the last P. Understanding how they arrived at the product and pricing - if not advising on those elements proactively - is critical.

I'm not the first to suggest the Four Ps aren't relevant. There were attempts to add three more Ps (People, Process, Physical Evidence). There are also dozens of models that have been introduced to replace it. For example, The Four C's. There are probably five models called the Four Cs that can be found. Professor Bob Lauterborn introduced his Four Cs in the early 1990s which updated the Four Ps with modern terms. Consumer Wants and Needs which replaces Product, Convenience to Buy which replaces Place, Cost to Satisfy standing in for Price and Communication for Promotion. Professor Koichi Shimizu authored his own updated version: Commodity, Cost, Communication, Channel.

Another version of the next Four Cs adds new dimension. Clarity means making your message simple and understandable. Consistency means reinforcing that simple message repeatedly to break through. Credibility means serving messages that consumers can find believable and worthy of paying attention to. Competitiveness means explaining how the brand or product is different or better than competitors.

Before we go too far with messaging nuance; however, let's look at overarching modes of communication. Today, there is a push towards the societal concept of marketing management (think: Toms Shoes or Even Stevens subs). Some brands are thinking more broadly about their message, a far cry from product or selling concept. **Product concept** says if we create something great, we will not need to market it. **Selling concept** says if we promote the hell out of our product we will drive sales. **Marketing concept** says

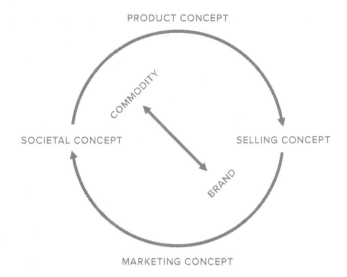

we should identify a consumer need and design products to meet that need. This is known today as product market fit. In the product concept, we are much more tactical and less focused on the brand promise. This usually applies to highly specialized products and markets today. **Societal concept** is most interesting because in essence it closes a loop back to a product focus, while hiding that fact in a brand message that is powerful to a specific audience.

Toms Shoes offers a powerful societal message. For each pair you buy (yes - you spoiled first-worlder) you trigger a donation to someone with no shoes. That is (was?) a powerful and unique value proposition. Could this work with a luxury car or private jet flight? Not likely. Because most of us don't consume those things, or think people are truly 'in need' of them. It wouldn't work for private jet flight, but might work for coach domestic air travel. Pay attention to the types of products and brands that use the societal concept. They are typically lower in the commodity chain. In fact, the first designs of Toms Shoes were on the plain side. I know I'm not supposed to say this, but they're ugly. People didn't buy them for looks. They bought them because compared to Keds or another utilitarian type of footwear, they served the same purpose, made a statement normally hard to share - and actually helped someone.

Ridesharing brands like Uber and Lyft would never be able to use the societal concept. Until maybe now. Initially, Uber was treated like a luxury; the private driver for everyone. In fact, the approach used was initially marketing concept, then transitioned to product concept. In Uber's case, 70% of the communication you've ever seen has been recruiting for drivers - not recruiting customers!

With the emergence of Lyft, Flywheel and dozens of other brands the time might be right for a rideshare brand to use societal concept. In fact, Lyft was initially conceived as a social good to reduce the number of cars (and their ecological damage) on the road but this hasn't made it into their consumer marketing as they've scaled.

Now that ride sharing has become widely accepted and commoditized, a brand could shift. For every ride, we donate to a transit service in Haiti or donate subway cards in inner cities. That might be a meaningful differentiator between Brand A and Brand B in this space.

What I'm describing is part of product positioning. How do

people think about the product in the context of their category. There are a lot of shoe brands, Toms is the one that gives back. There are a lot of rideshare brands, Uber is the evil one. Axe deodorant creates desirability for those who wear it but Degree keeps you drier longer, a factor in social acceptance.

Takeaway: All this is usually decided by the brand's marketing team before they brief you. Sometimes, the claim they ask you to make isn't very strong or might be true but isn't compelling. Make it your business to understand and have a point of view on how you will sell, based on what will motivate the audience.

JOY - PAIN = VALUE

To describe all the mental processes we make when we consider a brand I would have to write all about neuroeconomics. Luckily, Phil Barden already wrote *Decoded*. I'm OK with it if you want to put this down and go read (or re-read) it.

Back so soon? Great. To boil down what is critical for strategists to understand - different sets of mental operators drive the way we think as consumers. We essentially weigh the joy we will derive from a product. This is heavily skewed by our perception of the brand.

Once our brains score how much joy the thing will provide, we begin deducting points for pain. This could be things like high price, effort to buy or waiting for delivery. If the pain doesn't cut too far into the joy, we act. We click. We subscribe. We buy.

Inside an agency, there is often fierce debate about brand ads versus promotional ads. It's possible to do both, as many great restaurant brands have proven in their TV ads, with 25 seconds for branding and five seconds for the value or promotion.

But this goes further than the brand and the offer. People lose joy whenever they encounter friction. It's the reason behind the meme "Shut up and take my money." Starbucks has mastered reducing friction. Customers walk in, order, wave their phone and leave. Better yet, they order on the app before they arrive, pick up their drink and leave. It's no coincidence that sales increased shortly after they introduced this feature to their app. It reduced pain and increased value.

But, sales started to wane because there was different pain being caused. Non-users waiting while mobile orders were prepared ahead of theirs. A reduction in conversation and engagement with baristas due to technology. For non-users of the app, pain increased and value decreased.

Takeaway: It's pretty simple math. As you think about messaging in campaigns, find the right weight for increasing the joy and diminishing the pain. As you think about execution, find ways to make it easier for people to engage. Increase joy. Decrease pain. Whatever those may be to the end user.

SATISFACTION IS DUMB

Satisfaction isn't dumb. But it is a dumb thing to hang your hat on. A traditional measure of brand or product success is 'satisfaction.' This is often measured and reported by Consumer Reports and J.D. Power among others.

When you last ate at McDonald's (this is a safe space, you can admit it here) were you satisfied? Were your very basic needs and expectations met? Most likely yes. Great! Success for the brand! What if I asked if you to rank the experience at McDonald's on a scale from 1-10 with 10 being Nordstrom service with Lyft convenience and Houston's food? Still satisfied? Hmmmm.

What if I asked you the basic Net Promoter question - would you recommend this McDonald's based on this experience? Comparing the value of 'satisfied' customers to the value of Net Promoters tells us that satisfaction is baseline. If customers aren't satisfied you don't have a business. But it takes much more to sustain and grow.

Takeaway: Satisfaction was a common measurement device before brands began designing delightful experiences. Just satisfying customers means losing them soon. Design programs to overachieve and measure more significant indicators to prove success and brand growth. Satisfaction is now meaningless. Aim higher.

You don't need an MBA to think strategically about brand marketing. But you do need to understand the key concepts well enough to communicate and to know what they're trying to do. The concepts above are basic items that are often discussed on the brand side, and rarely mentioned inside the agency.

A lot of the foundational pieces of marketing don't make sense anymore given the way consumers find products. And the way consumers market for products on behalf of brands. But it's important to understand. Most musical virtuosos don't start that way. They learn the basics before breaking the rules and creating their own. Understand how marketing works so you can know how to bend it to your goals.

5. HOW CHOICE HAPPENS

I've just touched on the primary equation that brains compute when we consider products. Joy minus Pain. For an advanced look at how people compare and decide, Google 'Daniel Kahneman.' To get the basics of what you need to understand better than you do now, read on.

The very fundamentals you probably learned in school about marketing actually come from economists. It's been that way for 50 years. They created a model based on how they thought people might or should compare products in an ideal world. These are good models made on logical assumptions. So much of the work we still do is based on these models. The traditional shopper journey and the marketing funnel both come from these assumptions. But economists are weird. Which is why they don't make any sense.

When creating these models, economists supposed that we look at two or more products side by side every time we needed to buy a new tube of toothpaste and compared our options based on a checklist. Wow! Have you ever done that? Yes, I know that you have, once or twice. But usually for special purposes or categories you are buying for the first time like a car or a computer.

Some people smarter than me recognized that this just isn't the way people live in the world. It's too much thinking; more than the brain can handle. For most purchases consumers have a series of shorthand decisions they make subconsciously, and think very little about the rest based on some known quirks we all share. This field, known as behavioral economics, studies these tricks that drive decision making.

It's an ~~expansive~~ huge field that draws on expertise in a number of sciences. Reading about behavioral economics will lead you to elements of anthropology, cognitive and social psychology, neuroscience, sociology and beyond. Studies relating to behavioral economics are endlessly fascinating and can become a bit of a rabbit's hole for the curious. For the purposes of practical understanding I'm going to focus on some key concepts that relate to strategy in order to demonstrate how people choose.

Takeaway: People hate complex thinking. We don't want to think. The smaller or more inconsequential we deem the decision, the less mental energy we want to expend. Plan accordingly.

OK, that might be a little harsh. We do hate complex thinking but it's not our fault. It's evolution. Most of our thinking happens, well - without thinking. All the thinking we do has been classified into two levels by those who study psychology and neuroscience. The classification was popularized by Daniel Kahneman in his book *Thinking Fast & Slow*. He saw decision-making as two clear systems of thought.

Have you ever arrived at work and had no clear memory of your trip? That is System 1 thinking in action. System 1 guides all the fast, automatic and efficient decisions our brain doesn't want to waste energy on. We know where to turn left, where to slow down and where to park because we have trained ourselves over time. Our brain is then free to consider other decisions or to simply rest.

System 1 is implicit and imperfect. We jump to conclusions and lean on biases to cut down processing power. This is how you can end up surprised by what you just purchased at the grocery store when you empty the bags at home. You thought you were grabbing product A, but you didn't stop to think carefully or compare and you ended up with product B.

In reality, System 1 is the only way we can accomplish *anything* in our day without being frozen by choice. Evolution has given us some guides for major risks, if we don't detect any danger System 1 stays active and keeps us moving. But for situations that we need deeper consideration, there is System 2.

System 2 is what you used when you compared cars. It is deliberate and takes conscious effort. When we make a complex decision we opt to dedicate processing power to it. This might be used for a side by side comparison or a list of pros and cons. The effort is worth it - System 2 is more reliable as you would expect.

What's interesting is that you typically have a System 1 reaction to every decision. That's your primal brain powering through just another situation in your day. But something in your brain kicks in when you have to decide between jobs, or suddenly feel uncertain about which direction you should go to get back to your hotel.

When our brain is unstimulated it will stay in System 1 for as long as possible. Changes in environment or even in small details can activate increased focus: System 2. So how does our brain coast for so long in System 1?

Let's take a jargon break for the word '*heuristics*.' This is another big word that means points of comparison. When people make decisions they are looking for signposts to help them. Heuristics are those signposts that keep the brain moving efficiently. Now you know. You can use the word to sound smart or make it easy for people to follow you by choosing simpler words.

BOUNDED RATIONALITY

When economists built their consumer consideration model they assumed incorrectly that people treat all decisions equally. They also failed to factor time and other resources into their process. They were modeling a world with unlimited thinking about the brand of ground coffee.

Behavioral economics points out that people do have some limits to their thinking. People only have limited information. In the economists' 'perfect rationality' model, people know everything and decide based on a huge data set. Even with the internet, there is a limit to what we know about the choices we have, and a lot of the information is imperfect.

A second limitation is our brains. Like a computer, we have only so much processing power. We ration processing power based on the importance or perceived importance of the decision. Even when we attempt to apply thought, our focus is limited by the other things on our mind and the stimulus being pulled in.

Finally, time. We cannot imagine endlessly about the

benefits and costs of each brand of ground coffee. There are limits to their time. Like you there are many other things to get done in a day, this decision can't take all day. When we work on a campaign for a brand, it becomes a major focus of our day. For the consumer, the impression lasts 30 seconds. We tend to forget that people - even when grocery shopping - are making choices on another 50 items during their trip. This one is small at best.

Takeaway: Thinking isn't infinite. For most of the decisions we're working on, time will be even more limited. Make sure you are focusing your teams on the primary points (heuristics) that the audience will need to know to choose your brand.

THE BACKFIRE EFFECT

A group of researchers lead by Brendan Nyhan and Jason Reifler have studied the so-called 'backfire effect.' According to the research, someone with a strong belief on a topic will not be swayed by factual evidence that goes against that belief. They will actually react by rejecting the argument and fall back on their initial belief even more deeply. Facts that demonstrate their belief is wrong make them believe it more. They found this to be true with passionate issues like politics and religion. It doesn't apply to many brand decisions. It turns out people just aren't that passionate about orange juice.

An interesting sideline to the study is the way people process information on topics they have an interest and a belief in. If they hear a story and it is missing information or is incomplete in any way (which it always is according to bounded rationality), people are willing to accept mistruths to complete the story and support their belief. This is why fake news is so often shared by your Uncle Ned on Facebook. We look for things that reinforce what we believe and we reject things, even facts, that challenge them.

If you have been drinking Guinness since you turned 21 (and not a day sooner, I'm sure) you know that it is actually pretty light. Those who haven't drunk it believe it to be heavy and filling. They have heard the unattributed stories about hospitals giving it to patients in the UK to put weight on them. If you were to argue (factually) that Guinness has fewer calories, carbs and alcohol than regular Budweiser and Coors would people simply agree and become a brand fan? Would they even try it? What do you think it would take?

Many times, brand managers will believe that a simple set of facts about their brands will be a bullet proof case for category shoppers to switch brands. Instinctively, the creative team knows that a list of benefits - even if they are strong - will not convince anyone. Now you're starting to understand the science behind why. People don't want to think. They don't want to be convinced. And, they especially don't want to be told they're wrong.

Takeaway: To overcome the backfire effect, the indirect route will be more successful, according to the researchers. They suggest you avoid staging an argument. Instead, create a problem or puzzle to be solved together with your audience. Give them ways to find the answers on their own.

MENTAL ACCOUNTING

Thank Richard Thaler for this concept. The short version is this - people aren't always rational about their money. Even though all of a given consumer's money may draw from a single account, people mentally account for different types of purchases from that same account in different ways. They may assess the value of clothing as a future cost while assessing food as a current cost from the same account.

This is huge. Why? Because mental accounting is one of many mental excuses people allow themselves for overspending. Understanding how a given set of consumers weigh different purchases is valuable for knowing when and how to reach them with a given message.

For example, most consumers consider rent or auto ~~expenditures~~ payments higher order expenses than food or clothing. This means they put much more focus on decisions relating to their next car (or whether they should even have one) than they do on their lunch. Most consumers have framed the cost for lunch as minimal when compared to a potential car payment.

Takeaway: Framing is everything. People look for ways to compare costs as well as products. These comparisons might not be logical. A car payment has no natural comparison to your jeans. But people do make these associations in their mind. Strategists have the opportunity to find the cost comparison that is most advantageous to the brand.

FEEDBACK

We all receive feedback. Your boss tells you to rewrite your brief. Even with no more information you understand the work product was substandard, right? Markets receive feedback as an interpretation of sales or traffic data. Foot traffic has doubled? The newest campaign or offer is working. If sales are down, prices may be too high.

For decision making we use feedback for ongoing behaviors. Take a very common example - Dynamic "Your Speed" signs that we encounter on roads every day. They repeat information we can see on our own dashboard, yet when we see we are driving 49 in a 45 mile-per-hour zone, we usually tap the brakes, don't we?

Sound far removed from your work? It isn't. Look how good airlines are at reminding you of your current loyalty mileage and your distance from your next reward trip or promotion to a higher tier. That's no accident. Any loyalty-based business has added in feedback to inform consumers how they are doing in comparison to arbitrary or fictionalized competitive goals. Why do people care? Merely because they've seen a chart.

That is the power of feedback.

Takeaway: Figure out how to add feedback to your customer journey and quickly. We all want to know how we are performing, and we are all subject to peer norming. We rank ourselves against others or against rules. In the case of airlines, we are ranking ourselves against 'rules' that are totally arbitrary. There's no reason why one mileage level is better than another. And yet, people take extra flights to achieve status.

PRICE IRRATIONALITY

Holy crap, do we love things when they're free. People will choose less valuable items over competitors when the cheaper item is labeled as free. This may be no shock. But in his book Predictably Irrational, Dan Ariely's research proved that totally artificial numerical framing guided consumers to a specific value perception of a value. He crushed the idea of rationality. He had subjects provide the last digits of their social security number, then react to the price of an object. Those with the highest numbered social security cards (top 20%) were willing to pay nearly three times as much for an item (a cordless keyboard) as those with the lowest numbered social security ID. Do you follow? He got them to recite a random number, which affected the price they were willing to pay. The higher the number they read, the more they were willing to pay.

Well, that's a fine academic exercise. How does this play out in the marketplace? Brands tend to create a top tier item that is priced higher than common wisdom would dictate. Though many consumers may rule out that top priced item, they have a completely accepting perspective of the next item in the product mix. Consumers then think that item, priced at 80% of the top for example, is much more reasonably priced and therefore willing to pay. We've seen retailers like Target add premium products in store, presumably for this reason.

If you can't create a new product in the line, there is another option. In advertising, it's possible to put a product in the context of other higher priced items to ~~provide~~ give the impression that your product is more valuable and worthy of consideration in that set. It's also quite possible, given Ariely's research, to create completely artificial guideposts for pricing that will ease consumers up and reduce price sensitivity. A campaign that uses arbitrary numerical cues may serve to position the product's price as favorable against a set of meaningless numbers. At least that's what the research says.

Takeaway: People naturally compare numbers to other numbers. It's just how we're wired. But it's not always so natural since the numbers aren't necessarily related. Take advantage of this behavior when you can.

People are not great at assessing value. We make up a model in our mind of what we think something should cost and move from there. Sometimes this is just from an assumption of the cost we would like to pay, or the amount we have. We also tend to believe things are more valuable simply because we own them. A pencil costs three cents. You might guess the pencil in your drawer costs 10 if someone wanted to buy it from you. Just because it is already in the drawer. Odd, right? This is known as the endowment effect.

This extends to other behaviors. A study published by Michael Norton, Daniel Mochon and Dan Ariely (go read this, seriously) looked at the price of Ikea furniture versus its perceived value. They found that people assigned much higher value to furniture they assembled themselves than to the components before assembly - or after being disassembled! This valuation difference was also found in people's Lego creations and even simple origami.

I have no data to support this idea, yet I can't help but think about restaurants that offer high customization. One brand I worked with is a gourmet burger concept called The Counter, offering dozens of ingredients that can be combined in millions of unique ways. You can have a turkey burger with sprouts, gruyere, sweet and sour sauce on a whole wheat english muffin. Naturally, the price of the burgers is a bit higher. But consumers feel the value is there because they chose the combination that appealed to them in that moment, and believed their unique creation was superior to mass menu options sold in other quick serve and fast casual restaurants. Ironically, the most common order is a beef burger with american cheese on a regular bun. But consumers still felt it was more valuable than other burgers because they chose those basic ingredients themselves!

Scarcity bias is another way we create inflated value of a product. Have you ever noticed that there is one toy each holiday season that parents literally fight over? In 2016 it was Hatchimals, which my brother-in-law found via Craigsist for my kids after running out of options. He paid five times the retail price. Why? Because they weren't available at Toys 'R Us, Ebay or Amazon (and because he's extremely nice to my kids). Are these toys worth five times the value of other toys? I can tell you firsthand, they are not.

The low availability creates inflated value. This is from the classic relationship between supply and demand, which is rarely on display in its purest form. When we fear the item we seek will sell out, we overestimate its value. Airline websites use scarcity bias to drive shoppers to act right away. They often display a badge with the number of seats left at the current price. **Only two left!** I better get the credit card and book this trip! What Orbitz leaves out is whether other flights are more or less expensive. Consumers fill in the blanks and assume if it is scarce, it must be valuable and more likely to go up in price. Better buy now.

TIME

So much of our decision making has to do with the context of time. We tend to receive and store information differently depending on when we get it. Present bias describes our unwillingness to think accurately about the future. I call it now vs later. People are terrible at measuring the dollar value of their time. Need an example? Just look at savings rates of U.S. consumers over the past few decades. Though they've begun ticking back up, they should be much higher. There is no rational argument for not saving money for the long-term except, of course #YOLO.

We tend to value money now over money later, even when it's more money later. Study after study has proven that people will take a percentage of something offered later if they can have it today. People aren't easily able to project themselves in the future and therefore have a lower value of what they will need later. Therefore, we have to consider how we offer discounts and value to customers in relation to the present and the future.

This applies to much more than money. Diversification bias tells us how much we project we will want something later, based on our current emotions. Ever grocery shop hungry? Diversification bias is the reason you bought too many snacks. We stock up on things we want now, only to learn later we don't want those things quite as much.

The emotions you feel when you make a decision can drive the over- or under-investment in that decision. When we're angry, we think much differently than when we're calm. That's why most grocery or restaurant points of purchase try to create craving and food arousal interest. Choosing food from a resting mental state doesn't lead people to buy Limited Time Offers or extra soda. But seeing the soda flowing over perfectly cut ice cubes in a perfectly clean glass at the beach does.

The truth is that we're terrible at predicting what we'll need or how we'll feel. We predict future emotions based on past experience - memories. Memories are tricky to draw from because humans have been trained by evolution to remember highs and lows for the most part. Our experience is essentially the average of those highs and lows. If you think about your favorite hamburger place, it's become your favorite because like the value equation mentioned earlier, the good experience outweighs the bad. Because of this cumulative memory, you expect your next visit to the burger place to be equally memorable. When you actually go back to that burger place, it probably doesn't meet expectations. It can't because one visit can't compare to the sum of all of your past visits and experiences.

Inertia begins to bridge elements of time with social aspects of decision making. Because we're bad at predicting the future, we often over-inflate our current situation. Inertia prevents people from making decisions that require action or pain. That's why we don't want to save money today. We don't want to take action, especially if it requires thought.

Takeaway: Finding ways to inspire people to take the desired actions is not easy. Studies have proven that for the example of saving or starting a retirement fund, people are more likely to participate when the default selection opts them in, and they would need to take an action to opt out. This is not great for selling because opting people into a sale by default is unethical and a terrible customer experience.

SOCIAL

Another ~~vector~~ area influencing our decision-making is our complex social interactions. How we view other people and how we view companies are critical to understanding choice. Trust in other people is what keeps our society together and allows people to buy products. Environments rich in trust have proven to show better economic growth, productivity and workplace performance.

When people trust other people they can achieve superhuman tasks. When they get spooked and lose trust, it is nearly impossible to get it back. For brands, the implication is clear: don't shake trust. But when Volkswagen was hit with the scandal involving their diesel emissions reporting, they didn't lose trust for long. In fact, one year later they were near the top for global auto sales. Why? Because they spent 50 years building credibility and trust that overrode this single scandal. And because diesel emissions aren't a violation of consumer trust. For most drivers, they're a violation of trust between the brand and the government. In other words, had it been a scandal involving overestimates of miles-per-gallon that cost car buyers money, they would not have been back quite so quickly.

This is not a guess. This has been proven in research. When asked to choose between scenarios in which bad luck would be the same as being cheated, a research team lead by Bohnet, Greig, Herrmann, & Zeckhauser found that people widely favored the 'bad luck' scenario. People hate being cheated.

Traditional economists account for a certain amount of cheating in systems in which individuals ~~conduct commerce~~ buy and sell. It is anticipated for the individual gain within the system. Therefore, those economists theorize that consumers in an ideal system accept that cheating. But *behavioral* economists weight distrust more heavily. People take pains to avoid being cheated.

In fact, a series of experiments conducted by Ernest Fehr and Klaus Schmidt showed that people err towards equality over any other outcome. When subjects of their research were presented with the idea that opponents in a game may end up with more rewards, they made choices which lead them to earn less in an effort to prevent their opponents from earning more.

This is why Tom's shoes appeal to us. It seems fair. We're getting something we want and those who can't are given something too.

People crave fairness in any environment. This comes from evolution as studies with monkeys have shown. Sarah Brosnan and Frans de Waal found that monkeys preferred receiving no reward of food than to have another monkey in the test group given more. They were visibly angered at the person distributing the rewards when another monkey received more.

Ever seen the person next to you at a restaurant get a better plate of food, even though you ordered the exact same thing? How did you feel about it? There, there. It's natural. Capuchin monkeys feel the same way. Keeping up with the Joneses is alive and well, it's just gotten more complicated. We might be angry with the Joneses, or with the people or companies (or government rules) that we perceived help them stay ahead.

It used to be that a tenet of classic consumer packaged goods advertising was reporting directly - via advertising - that yours is a 'trusted brand.' But about 20 years ago, people stopped taking companies' words for it.

We have seen public relations, word of mouth and social media all become more important ways to reach consumers. This is now spiking with the trend towards influencer marketing. Consumers are simply more likely to trust peers than a company.

In a 2016 study by Influence Central, 80% of respondents said they often seek peer opinions while 59% turn to experts, and women value first-hand experience over any other reason for the recommendations they receive. Take this with a grain of salt, however, because the study is by a company that sells influencer marketing. But the point is clear. Over the course of 2017, we've seen campaigns with micro-influencers outperforming those influencers with big followings. Why? I believe that people are beginning to get suspicious of 'celebrity' influencers who have become brands in their own right.

Influencers efficacy with consumers is based on our trust biases. But they also touch on another facet of behavioral economics - social norms. We observe what is 'normal' or acceptable behavior and apply those rules to our own conduct. We figure out where the line between polite and rude behavior is. This is also how we develop a sense of style, and what is cool. Influencers serve as examples of trends and we decide if we want to ~~emulate~~ copy or reject that example.

Social norms are not static. In the black and white era (even before my time), air travel required a suit and hat; gloves for the ladies. Been on a flight lately? People show up in sweatsuits, leggings or in pajamas with pillow in tow. So we see that social norms can change and bend based on the context. How you dress for a dance club is different than for a wedding. But even wedding attire is different by region of the world or country, time of year, or time of day.

The evolution of norms is the cause for the generational gap. As a Gen Xer, I was irritated with articles written by Baby Boomers during the early part of my career that described us as slackers. Where have we read that same line of bullshit recently? Oh, that's right. In the trillions of articles about those snowflake Millennials.

Social norms also paint our understanding of gender roles. During my lifetime, I've seen the dramatic rise in acclaim for female athletics. When I say UConn basketball, you probably think of the women's team first. The UFC promoted Ronda Rousey over hundreds of male fighters to reach mainstream audiences. These too change over time, don't they? Society's perceptions of gender and sexuality evolves. As recently as the 1980s gay men were played for comic relief. Ellen Degeneres was run off of network television for playing a character that came out of the closet. America wasn't ready. Today, many Americans applaud Caitlyn Jenner. That's a sea change in social norms.

That's not happening in the media alone. Norms change because we change. You have probably noticed more and more CPG and general ads moving away from the 'dad is a dummy' formula to the stay-at-home dad as matter of fact formula. Fathers are expected to be more in touch with their children and participate more than previous generations. We see more stay-at-home dads. We begin to accept the social norm. Brands follow.

The same with products. More men wear what we used to consider makeup than ever. Now identified as 'product' by the cosmetics industry - eyeliner, concealer and other items are gaining new acceptance by males.

We long to fit in with our social groups. We believe that we do and make choices we believe are consistent with who we are within the group. I'm not suggesting that if my peers begin wearing eyeliner I might consider buying some to fit in, but I might buy a pair of ~~more aesthetically appealing~~ hipper, cooler Toms. In the past, trends moved down in age groups, but today styles of younger people are influencing older people. Gen Xers and Boomers are more comfortable borrowing from Millennials and Gen Y.

was it not always this way

Sometimes we make choices that conflict with how we see ourselves. It could be something small like buying a brand out of the norm or bigger - like acting in self-interest or greed. This action confuses us because we want to believe we are steady and reliably part of our group.

The action goes against our belief. When we face this confusion, we're experiencing cognitive dissonance. We've done something that doesn't align with our own perception of who we are and the group to which we belong. Our response is rationalization. We invent the reason after the fact for why it was OK to behave the way we did. We might do some research on reviews to validate a purchase, for example.

Most people think they are good with money. Even more people aren't very good with money. Most of those people who aren't good with money have no idea how they mismanage theirs. They rationalize their spending habits - or each individual purchase outside their budget. Brands like Mint and Acorns introduced products that help these people visualize their money habits or save effortlessly to provide actions that better align with their beliefs. These brands aren't playing against weaknesses caused by dissonance, they are actually making it possible for customers to realign to our desired role in our groups. Powerful indeed.

When we market a brand that doesn't deliver with the practical experience we can create dissonance for our customers. This happens when movies show one experience in the trailer that differs from the actual 90 minutes on the screen. People think, 'I would never have come to this type of movie' and leave disappointed or angry. This is why I never make service part of a strategy. It's too easy to under-deliver on service, and easy for customers to get frustrated with the brand.

The buzzwords or the behaviors named by sociologists aren't all that important. The concepts are. Understanding why we make choices is critical to designing strategies to win those choices and to guiding our clients to business success.

6. THE THREE PHASES OF STRATEGY

When thinking about how strategy personnel operate with brands, it's not easy to define where people step in and out of the business. At Santy, our strategy team is probably more involved with clients on a day-to-day basis than at most agencies our size. We hire smart, curious people who are driven to improve business for our clients and love thinking about it. It's hard to pull them away from a client because we've found that re-engaging them is not efficient. Having a subject matter expert who is always on is just simpler and more productive for our clients.

To simplify the organization of strategic process, I break down engagements into three phases. As you can tell from above, we rarely execute in phase order (or in any order). In a perfect world, we start at the beginning and walk a strategic path with a client and see it through. The marketing world is far from perfect. Here is the ideal anyway because you have to start somewhere.

The first phase is what I refer to as Foundational. This is all the work we do when we onboard a new client, or when we build a new product strategy. This is essentially starting from scratch. What would we do if this was a brand new company? The main deliverable here is a comprehensive brand brief.

Next is the Campaign phase. This is when the client brings a brief to launch a campaign of some sort to drive an action. In this phase we employ what we learned in phase one and layer specifics about the client's objectives for the initiative. Here's where we write a creative brief.

Finally, we get to Phase III; Post. The post phase has our team looking at our results to determine performance and really striving to find new information to better inform the brand brief or thinking for the next campaign. The output here might only be internal, building data for our next campaign.

Now that I've shared the three phases, I'm going to add a caveat. We rarely get the opportunity to work this way. Or at least, most clients don't subscribe immediately to the complete list I'll lay out for you. However, this is the ideal. I'm also breaking up the order a bit to simplify the logic. I'll be touching on brand as part of the campaign phase only so it follows customer understanding, since customers define the brand in their mind, not the company.

You'll also note quickly that research is part of all three phases. Traditionally, agencies have used research like focus groups to test a campaign idea during Phase II. I'll describe how research in different forms can be used throughout all three phases to improve the output.

7. PHASE I: FOUNDATION

The foundational phase is where all the work we do to understand the brand and competitive environment takes place. Everything we do here sets the stage for future work, so small mistakes can be magnified into huge problems. A buzzword I absolutely hate is "data-driven." This phase is not about being "data-driven," because everything is now data-driven, which merely means that there are people looking at data. Busy work.

The Foundation Phase is mission-driven. You are the strategist. You are using data, yes. But using it to chart a course for this brand. Do not lose sight of this. The goal is to use past and present data to look into the future and outline opportunities based on probabilities derived from facts.

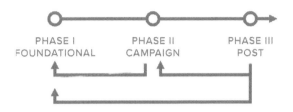

We break the Foundation phase into two related aspects. There is obviously the brand side of things, which entails understanding all the nuances of audience, perception and messaging, etc. The second part is often not a part of agency strategy work, but is critical: the business side. We usually leave this to our counterparts on the brand side, but it's important work that must be done either in collaboration with clients or on our own if we are to provide value to them.

If we are going to have a solid understanding of their business and help them find opportunities, we need to look at everything. Earlier, I split the brand and business to make a point. There is no separation from a customer's perspective. The decisions that drive a business to cut costs are reflected in the end product or the final experience received by that customer, thus affecting the brand. As you well know, it is all connected.

To have the full picture we have to understand the relationships between the wider business environment and external factors, the competitor offering and strengths and the customer desires and drivers. Your best strategy will come (and your best agency work will be sold) when you can demonstrate that you understand how each of these things affects the others. Sounds complicated, but it doesn't have to be.

We start with a look at competitors. There are a lot of aspects to this work, so let's start where consumers do. Researching competitors should be an immersive activity. Shop the competitor yourself to see how they operate, understand their value proposition and look for similarities and differences between each company. Pay attention to the customers, the overall traffic. In the case of a CPG or non-retail brands, use reviews and social listening to inform your understanding of who is buying and what they think of each product.

As you consider competitors, think about why each might be chosen or passed up. A win/loss analysis is a way to understand drivers and advantages of each player, post-purchase. If you ask people inside each company, they'll have their own perspective on why they did or didn't win a specific customer.

For example, if you are working on an auto brand like Ford and ask different internal people why consumers bought Toyota, the engineer will say engineering. The designer will say design. The person responsible for selecting the trunk latch, will likely say the choice has something to do with the trunk. The salesperson will say price (every time). You can't assemble a cohesive narrative from those collected anecdotes because nothing matches up. Instead, talk to customers after they've chosen and find out why they selected. They'll give you more insight based on their real motivations and reactions throughout the process.

There are so many powerful tools out there to help bring more shape to the competitive intelligence your client needs. Let's go deeper. First, plot each competitor on a value grid. A value grid helps visualize the ways consumers see the marketplace when they shop.

Identifying how the competitive set looks to consumers in terms of value will help you craft everything from your brand promise to your digital strategy. To take this from theoretical to useful, plot your local grocery stores on the value grid. You should not be surprised to see how neatly they fall into specific spots on the grid. Every town has the top right boutique grocery, the low cost, low value option and the middle-of-the-road parity player. This helps you understand where your client lives, how they should be

MORE COST	*less for more* HOLLOW PROMISES	*same for more* FADING STAR	*more for more* PREMIUM POSITIONING
SAME COST	*less for same* TAKING THE PISS	*same for same* PARITY PLAYER	*more for same* VALUE LEADER
LESS COST	*less for less* BUDGET OFFERING	*same for less* VALUE DRIVER	*more for less* VALUE BREAKER

communicating to their customers and the types of experiences they should be offering.

Spend time on each of their websites to see how they are messaging and begin formulating ideas about their approach to customer experience. You will start noting the brand promise of each as you interpret it throughout your exposures. One of the first things you will create is a series of perceptual maps. You will plot the aspects of the category most important to the core customer on cross axes and define the space each brand occupies. You're using details of each brand's service, pricing and offering to get to higher order perceptions by consumers. What do the customers think?

In the sample graphic, I've used pretty generic labels on the axes. Getting those right takes some effort. When designing perceptual maps for a brand, we will often draft a dozen or so using different labels on each axis to determine the most useful options. Here, useful means meaningful to consumers and actionable to the client. As always, the more specific you can get with the descriptors, the more powerful the map will be. There is such a thing as too specific. If Domino's had a perceptual map for the pizza category, one label would be 'convenience' but probably not 'great mobile app.'

It's simple to plot perceptual maps but difficult to perfect them. Our own anecdotal understanding may steer how we plot brands on a map, so using research is key. Focus groups are great for gathering feedback on the overall perceptions, when applicable. Online community studies will provide more detailed information and give participants a chance to think and respond over a few days, giving you more information to work with.

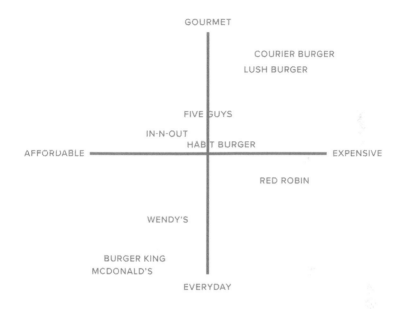

This cursory look at the competitive group will provide context for the rest of your work. Look at your client's product and determine what stage of life it is in. There are dozens of ways to assess this. Here are a few effective ones.

THE FIVE FORCES MODEL
Michael Porter mapped out a simple, but powerful model for deeper understanding of the marketplace in 1979. The five forces model provides a way to examine the competitive environment and identifies ways to win. I've rarely heard it talked about by agency folks but consultants and other professionals in business intelligence use it as a core concept.

Porter found the process not only useful for developing the strategic plan, but also critical to understanding the structure of the industry. Nothing happens in a vacuum, but for some reason we expect strategy for our clients to work that way. The five forces allows us to have a look around the world our client's business inhabits and map out the wider context. It's impossible to make decisions without that context. Or at least, intelligent decisions. I'm including the five forces model as a way to inform other avenues of understanding needed to have a context in line with those of your clients.

The first force is competitive rivalry. This force looks at the intensity of the competition in the industry, but goes beyond the traditional. We start with the known category players and examine their offerings, pricing and customer base. When we describe rivalry, it's considered high if there are few players, product or category parity and low or no barriers to prevent customers from switching brands. The cola wars are a great example of high competitive rivalry in an industry. Two big players, nearly identical products and ease of switching. In this environment, advertising and price wars often occur.

The bargaining power of suppliers is force two. As in any industry, and in the first force, competition drives cost. This goes levels and levels deep. Apple has a potential problem with screen manufacturers because suppliers are rare. The fewer suppliers, the more control they have over pricing.

This is why the DeBeers Corporation goes to such lengths to

control the supply of diamonds. They're the only supplier so they get to keep costs high. If you're a manufacturer that uses diamond for your product, profitability is threatened by the control DeBeers has. If they raise prices, you are forced to choose between raising prices of your own product or cutting margins.

Force number three is the bargaining power of customers. When there are many brands in a category, and high ease of switching as identified in competitive rivalry. Customers can impact pricing, especially when they are an in-demand or smaller audience. This all relates back to the laws of supply and demand. Many options for consumers usually drives down cost and makes business harder and less attractive.

Mattresses are an example of an industry that has suffered from increased bargaining power of customers. Going back 10 years, there were only a few players locked into tight distribution deals and (overly high) prices. But advances in materials, production, shipping and distribution via the internet has loosened the choke hold of Sealy and Serta. Customers rarely need to buy in this category, and they finally have some control, which they are happily exercising. A handful of foam mattress brands have broken through, thanks to renewed bargaining power of consumers. Leesa, Tuft & Needle, Loom & Leaf, Lull; too many to count. Now, prices are coming down as competition has increased bargaining power of customers.

As with industry attractiveness, we also look at the ability for other companies to enter the market. Force number four is the ability of new entrants. Especially today, this is a huge concern, which is often (always?) overlooked. See: Amazon buys Whole Foods. What other companies or brands could enter the market we're examining?

Using our cola example, Virgin entering the market was a splashy move based on their understanding of the marketing and distribution needed to compete. Ultimately failing in US markets, they did well in the early stages. The critical piece for strategists is to look at the marketplace and investigate what other brands could make a move to enter the market. Not easy to do, but necessary to protect brand and business interests over the long term. Most companies don't look for indirect models. Look at your client's business and make some educated guesses about who may enter their category based on similar audiences, distribution, products or supply chain.

In the same vein is our final force - the threat of substitutes. Once, Blackberry was a powerful company because of the uniqueness of its flagship product. It's barely mentioned anymore. Why? Touchscreen smartphones from Apple and Google's partners et al replaced it. So, why did consumers switch? The product was superior and offered at a competitive price point through intelligent distribution with mobile carriers. In Apple's case, they also built a unique supplier network that kept Blackberry from making any defensive moves. If you remember, the co-CEOs of Blackberry dismissed the iPhone because of battery life and security deficiencies - core strengths of their device. They didn't understand that people would be willing to make that substitution for a touchscreen experience. "We'll be fine," Jim Balsillie was quoted as saying.

The five forces model helps fill in the context, but it leaves out partnerships and strategic alliances. It's also just the model, and importantly does not include guidance for action. That's where you come in. None of these tools mean anything on their own. They have strength when you tie tools together with marketing prowess to draw conclusions. When competitive rivalry is high, advertising needs to stand out. Niche markets create more power for the brand, so you need to figure out ways to put your client in a niche or to emulate one.

STEEP ANALYSIS

A great way to gain perspective on the market is to conduct a STEEP analysis (also known as PEST and several other variations). Yup, an acronym; Social, Tech, Economical, Ecological, Political. Looking at the market from these five directions tells you what is happening and what is possible. This initial context will be very useful for your brand brief and for understanding how the market may change.
To help bring STEEP to life, let's run through an analysis for electric car and engineering brand Tesla.

SOCIAL:

The initial product strategy attracted a wealthy user base and positioned the product as premium. Traditional eco-consumers favored the Prius, but upscale buyers came to Tesla for the prestige, a part of their stated strategy to move

63

downmarket. Acceptance for electric vehicles has grown in the US and abroad, while Tesla has introduced lower priced products more accessible to the masses.

TECHNOLOGY:
Tesla has innovated with battery, charging and self-driving features making their line desirable and ahead of trends. Major carmakers haven't figured out how to make and market a comparable vehicle in the US yet. The Prius outperforms on efficiency but underperforms on power, a sacrifice many Americans are not yet ready to make. Tesla shared its patents publicly, a move that demonstrates the brand's commitment to improving tech for electric cars and renewable energy. Tesla's early self-driving technology positions the brand well with the trend of autonomous vehicles replacing traditional cars.

ECONOMIC:
The growing market for electric cars and batteries means Tesla's promise of lower cost cars is coming true. With many states still offering incentives for electric vehicles and for alternative power sources that return power to the grid, the time may be right for mainstream adoption in the next 18 to 24 months. On the commercial side, manufacturing facilities are in demand in the US, with individual states competing with subsidies and other tax incentives to take the sting out of the start-up costs.

ECOLOGICAL:
Fossil fuels are widely accepted to be passé. Electric power has fewer damaging effects on the environment and is

gaining consumer appeal on a mass market level. However, the ecological costs of manufacturing batteries may offset some of the fuel benefits. Long term, the eco-damage may be less severe, but regulators and consumers have a lot to learn about these benefits.

POLITICAL:

It is a challenging time for innovation in the automotive space because the big players are well entrenched with government lobbyists. Each of the big automakers and oil companies is invested in existing models and working on legislation to extend the service lives of current vehicles. Pressure is on for politicians and candidates to demonstrate commitment to voters on ecological issues and change.

THE BOSTON MATRIX

The Boston Matrix, made famous by Boston Consulting Group (those consultants sure get creative with the names, don't they?) helps you understand the market opportunity, appropriate investment level and messaging style. What you are trying to learn is the relationship between the market growth rate and market share. This will get you to potential. Market growth rate = using revenue. Market share = making revenue. You'll have to find or be able to develop rough estimates of revenue and market share for each competitor. This will enable you to see the complete size of the market and the role your brand is playing.

The best products are referred to as 'stars' and are in the high growth, high income quadrant. As you invest, you have the potential for strong returns with an established product.

Strong moves with media and messaging with stars will pay dividends. Go big. An example of a star category is job boards. There is no limit to the growth potential of that market because people will always be looking for new jobs, and there is no reason a new player couldn't introduce a new dominant brand.

'Dogs' are the opposite of stars. Dogs aren't generating money and there isn't strong market growth, meaning major investing will have to happen to even hope for profit. Don't go all in on media here. Messaging will have to be innovative to break through and earn awareness. Laptops are dogs as a category. Competition and substitution is high and differentiation is hard earned.

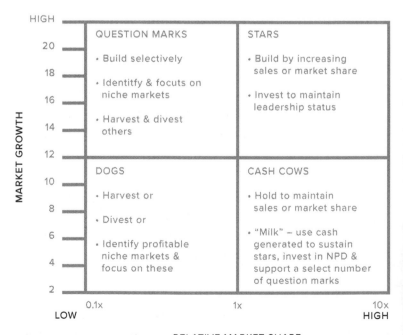

RELATIVE MARKET SHARE
(TO THAT OF THE LARGEST COMPETITOR)

Look for 'cash cows,' the businesses that are in low market growth areas but generating a lot of cash through outsized or growing market share. These products usually have high awareness and are churn and burn brands for campaigns. Reminders and trigger media will keep revenue coming in. Smart phones are a cash cow category. The market is mature and overall growth is maxed out in the United States. Brands are just reminding consumers to upgrade. And we do. Every 2.2 years.*

'Question marks' provide the biggest risk and reward. These are products or businesses with low market share in a high growth market. A competitor to Airbnb would be a question mark because it would undoubtedly play a challenger role in a market that Airbnb is growing almost single handedly. It's possible that Homeaway or another new competitor could enter and grow with the market as more people adopt home sharing as a practice.

Here you'll also need to consider where the product is in its lifecycle. The four major stages are Introductory, Growth, Maturity and Decline. Messaging and investment would obviously differ in the growth and decline phases, but by how much depends on where the business falls in a Boston Matrix. A cash cow in decline is still worth some media spend, as long as you are monitoring sales and market trends to know where the end of the line is.

MCKINSEY'S 9 BOX

A similar tool, McKinsey's 9 Box helps evaluate how a business looks from a market perspective. I like it because

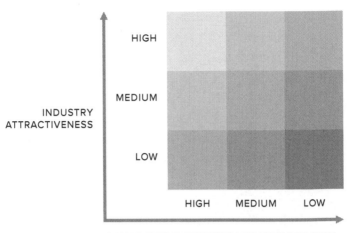

INDUSTRY
ATTRACTIVENESS

COMPETITITVE STRENGTH OF BUSINESS UNIT

it's a little simpler than the Boston Matrix. McKinsey actually developed this tool to be easily understood across a decentralized corporation. The goal of both is similar, help companies figure out where to invest.

The 9 Box breaks down two simpler axes. First, how attractive is the industry? How many companies are currently in, and how many will want to get into this business? Attractiveness is usually driven by potential for profitability or consumer interest. Most companies (except Amazon) won't enter a market for revenue, only for profitable revenue. If it's a new industry, only brands with adjacent business units are viable in most cases. As you know, a blue ocean environment is rare, but you'll also want to think about what other companies would have an interest or the ability to quickly enter this market. This takes a little imagination.

For example, Soda Stream is the leader in the custom carbonation category. But what if Coca-Cola decided to extend their freestyle line to a line of syrup pods à la Green Mountain Coffee's Keurig? That makes sense from a brand perspective, but the hardware would be a cost investment that might be too big a barrier to cross. Seeing who could enter, and how easily they could get there helps know how to invest marketing funds.

The second axis measures the competitive strength of the business unit. If it gets to be a crowded market, does your brand have any unfair advantages? How can they edge out competitors. This gets to the heart of the unique selling proposition. We're always optimistic our clients will be highly competitive, but it's often not the case.

SWOT ANALYSIS

The final tool I'll describe is one that is criminally underused and misunderstood. SWOT has been around forever. For some reasons, agencies just skip right over it despite its universal usefulness and simplicity. This tool takes no real data. It can be executed by one person and provides immediate actionable ideas.

For those familiar with SWOT, skip to the next paragraph. If not, don't be embarrassed about not knowing what it is. As I said, most agencies skip it. SWOT stands for Strengths, Weaknesses, Opportunities and Threats.

We conduct SWOT exercises in two steps. Step one is the traditional parts: listing out the internal and external items

SWOT STEP 1.

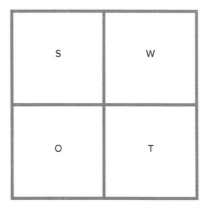

that fill out each of the four parts on a quartered grid. I recommend conducting SWOT exercises as a meeting in which ideas are compiled and debated as opposed to a traditional 'brainstorm' format. Brief people at an earlier kickoff meeting or via email and get their ideas prior to your SWOT regroup.

You'll use the regroup time choosing more meaningful ideas versus gathering lists, which is just less valuable. Especially when you involve most brand personnel, but also with some agency folks, the first ideas are often very soft. Companies tend to overinflate their strengths and underestimate their threats if they notice them at all. Be prepared to dig in and be aggressive about ruling out ideas that aren't thoughtful or meaningful.

It's also important to organize ideas into broader groups. You might consider grouping items in each quadrant by

SWOT STEP 2.

	O	T
S	SO	ST
W	WO	WT

competition, audience, media, distribution - or by another schema such as the five forces. When I've seen SWOT exercises completed, they almost always end with four lists of ideas. But this is just the beginning.

The misunderstanding about SWOT is that the lists are meaningful. They're not. As with most of the tools described in this chapter, we are trying to match the internal resources with the external environments to build an offense and a defense. That's why SWOT only works when people with diverse viewpoints are used. Different perspectives lead to better context. We involve people from the client team, but we try to add personnel beyond the marketing team. Five accountants would point out a detailed SWOT about accounting, but probably leave out a lot about consumer experience and product quality.

The output of that step is essentially four lists. Some items may make immediate sense as to what action to take, but most won't be so clearly linked to an action. Step two of a useful SWOT employs another component. To achieve some actionable takeaways, go one step further by comparing the items to finder larger themes and tighter insights.

This is done by creating a second quartered graph matching the internal and external pieces. It might not be immediately intuitive, but the Opportunities and Threats will tend to be external items while the Strengths and Weaknesses will be internal ones. Your second chart will have SO, WO, ST and WT boxes. By cross referencing the four groups you will see steps that need to be taken to address your client's soft spots and leverage their power.

8. PERSONAS

No successful business exists without customers. No business that exists will excel without thoroughly understanding those customers. When I talk to clients about their customers, I drive them to decide on who their top customers are. They are always quick to name their average customer. But it's more important to identify the very top. As in "If your business lost 90% of its customers, who should remain so that you could build on them?"

Think about that.

Nobody enjoys thinking about the ~~decimation~~ shrinking of their customer base. But understanding where they would put their chips if it happened tells you about their internal beliefs. Who drives sales? Your goal is to understand those top customers. It might be more than 10 or 15% of your customers. It might ultimately be more than one customer type for thriving businesses that make up different segments. That's a good problem to have.

Most brands know their customers. As a strategist you can learn a lot from your clients. From the inside, they observe things you just won't have access to unless you dig. The best businesses and marketing teams will be able to pull this information together to describe their customers in detail. That's where personas come in. What personas provide is an actual person (or people) the agency can design work to appeal to. Well, not an 'actual' person. A persona is a fictionalized person that is based on real data.

Why is it better to create a person to target instead of the median of data points? If I told you to buy a Mother's Day card for any mom, it would take you about 11 seconds to choose one. Find the Mother section in the card aisle, grab a card. This one should work. Or you might spend a few seconds finding a card that reflects your sentiment or style. Now, what if you were buying a card for your own mother? The type of thought you'd expend would be deeper. You know what buttons to push to make your mother happy. The more specific, the better.

When we start talking specifics there is a tendency to go to anecdotes. We start matching the attributes provided in a brand brief with people we know. This is natural and unavoidable. Fight against the urge to lock in on your ~~anecdotal~~ personal connection unless you have proven it with data.

Explore and find all the details you can about this best audience and understand their interests and drivers. If that matches the contact that came to mind, all the better, but locking in is dangerous. For starters, it's limiting. If you think you know the answer you will never search as completely. This is confirmation bias at its finest.

Going back to marketing, the key to great work is to define those customers. 'Define' goes way beyond demographics. Sure, 35-44, household income (HHI) $70k-80k, Married, 2.3 children, 1.2 pets could tell us a lot when there were far fewer ways to reach consumers. I don't value demographics much, so be careful with jumping to conclusions here. Instead, I subscribe to a model called life stages.

If we think about a group of 100 women aged 25-34 we might make some mental leaps. But what if I told you 10 of the women are in graduate school and working part-time? And that another 25 of the women have children? Do we think those two subgroups have the same outlook on life or interests? Taking it further, mothers of young children are more alike than mothers of grown children, or even children in elementary school. I may have more in common with someone who's out of my age group if they have children close in age to mine. Or more in common with older people if I have recently retired and now engage in the same activities.

Using zip code data provided by the U.S. Census, you can get a sense of the neighborhoods your target occupies. Or can you? We jump to some serious conclusions when we see a median HHI. Our own experience creates bias. Just like the consumers shopping for our products don't want to think, we use shortcuts to make decisions. It doesn't mean you're lazy. It's natural to land on a judgment. The job is to push through those biases and challenge yourself to find the right data.

INTERESTS

Today, we organize around interests. In my twenties I connected with people around music. Friends I have now I met coaching my son's soccer team. Our common interest in the kids and their team gave us a reason to connect. It's never been easier for people to find others who have a passion for their specific interests - no matter how obscure (e.g., Bronies). Interest-based data has replaced geographic data in a sense because we don't cluster around zip codes anymore, but around these interests which help us visualize the life stage of the persona.

We have to dig deeper to find out what makes this person tick. Creating a great persona is similar to great characters in novels and movies. We get to know them, their likes and dislikes. Their dreams and fears. Where are they sharing these, you ask? Sure they might report the basics for the census, but how am I supposed to get into their head? Start with social media. We share A LOT.

You can audit the Facebook audience to see how the brand's subscribers match up with your demographic description. You can also conduct a social listening exercise to see what people are saying about the brand and category. You'll want to go beyond the category to understand their preferences in other categories. From this listening, you can create segments based on attitudes - people who buy the brand grudgingly, people who love the brand, people who think the brand is expensive. Look at posts to understand usage patterns like day of week or time of day. When they're using tells a lot about how they think about a brand.

For one restaurant chain I audited, I found there was no statistically significant day or time that got more posts on social by users. This was a bar heavy concept with a beer and whiskey focus. There should have definitely been an increase on Friday and Saturday nights, maybe even Thursday. But comments were pretty much flat every day, across lunch and dinner. People didn't know how to use the brand. Compare that to Subway which sees huge spikes in comments every weekday from 11:40 a.m. to 1 p.m.

Once you have attitude segments around usage created, you can go back to Facebook or Twitter to find the interests and behaviors of the users who meet those attitudes. For example, you might find your social subscribers also follow the accounts of coupon or sweepstakes sites. We can make some intelligent guesses about their behaviors when we add that information to the demographics. It's also interesting to look at what other brands they follow. Are they exclusive within brand or product categories? If they follow entire categories, they might be interested in the subject (like runners) or shopping for coupons and deals (like department stores). Do they follow premium or value brands?

Now we're adding to the skeleton of the initial demographics. You will also be able to confirm or reset behavioral guesses provided by clients. We're able to see some of the shortcuts they take when they choose products. It is especially helpful to look at their behavior in categories beyond yours. If you're building personas for a CPG, look at the audience behavior in dining and services. You'll get a much fuller picture of the choices they make and who you are talking to.

Here it is useful to conduct surveys or even focus groups to understand attitudes. I don't believe in focus groups for creative testing unless the client is willing to test at scale. In other words, the total audience for a television buy will be in the millions, so let's not let 12 people in one market decide if the work is good or bad. But for persona building, groups are valuable because you can hear how they behave and some of the reasons why. Conversation can bring out the reasons why people behave the way they do.

BEHAVIORS
Now it's time to dive into media. First, look at the performance of past campaigns. How does your persona

respond to different media? This means studying campaign analytics to understand what kinds of messages drive the most action. You will need to have segmented data here to ensure you're looking at the right group of customers. In traditional media and broad digital campaigns it may be hard, but you should be able to narrow down digital campaigns through website analytics.

Because email lists are segmented and carefully curated, those campaigns should have a lot of rich information about messaging behaviors. Social content and ads are also informative because of the targeting provided by Facebook, Instagram and LinkedIn. It's clear which messages drive the most engagement and purchases (if applicable) with your target. These channels may also reveal additional audiences that react to your brand or messages.

Is the audience waiting for offers? Do they get excited by new products? Are they clicking when offered 'exclusives?' You should be seeing some patterns emerge.

The other half of our media work is determining what other media they consume. We know based on analytics where they are coming from online as a first step. But looking to tools like Scarborough or CubeYou can help us uncover their broader habits. When you tie this together with the things they follow on social media, you get a full picture of their interests and their habits. How they spend their time. What they care about. From combining those things you should be able to understand what drives them.

Media is an undervalued source of information. Yes, Nielsen or Scarborough will tell you how much time they spend listening to radio or streaming audio (or approximated on aggregate). But that's not all you get. If they watch very little TV, we can make some estimations about their lifestyle. When we combine that with information about their average commute time, and whether they drive or take public transportation, we learn more. We can understand based on income and commute time how to weigh time against money. People short on time will often pay premiums for things that make time or quickly provide "quality" time.

The work you've done so far covers their entertainment and their interests. The first step to build a persona is to edit the most common findings. Because you are dealing with populations, you will have to decide which things are of interest to your target persona and which things you leave out. Strategy is about sacrifice. Use your experience to have a point of view that makes your personas dimensional. That means they love some things, but hate others. And it isn't always stereotypical combinations. Not every fan of the NFL loves pizza and Bud Light. Fans of easy listening radio sometimes like UFC.

Spending time with all the data you've collected will help bring this person to life. The next part of creating this person is to give them a name. Look at actual names from your research. Focus group participants, Facebook subscribers. The name you select should reflect their name and upbringing. Choose a name that ~~encapsulates~~ feels like the personality of this character. When we work on assignments for our clients, we actually say "What would Allison think of this work?" We know she's not real, but we work to make sure she would appreciate what we're doing if she were. Assigning the persona a name makes it real. It turns the write-up from an it to a he or she.

Next, we write an essay to describe a day in the life of our persona that makes sense of all the statistics and data we've sifted through. Imagine them waking up. What time is it? Did the alarm wake them? Are they self-starters? Did the kids or dog run in and get them out of bed? At each point, we get to know our persona a little better and make them a little more real. We get specific with the choices he or she makes in a day and we explain why they did it. For one persona description I wrote "she chooses organic food, but she doesn't know why." More telling than the made-up reason I would have invented and based on an insight we had found - sentiment about 'organics' was highly positive but understanding was murky at best.

And that's the point. Personas are valuable because they are the summation of the facts about a population. When you find yourself torn on a piece of data or, more importantly, on a theme, it is probably time to add a persona. Usually, we add a persona when we find a different use for the product. Sometimes, we do create specific personas for unique media behaviors. Having fewer personas is more focused and better for campaign development.

It is up to you, the author of the persona's story to make sure they remain a living, breathing thing. You want to present the persona to any stakeholders and get buy in, because everything you do going forward should pay off for this 'person,' just like the card you bought for your own mother in the earlier example. When you think about the brand or the product, it is up to you to include the latest version of the persona in the brief.

Like most of the work you do, the persona is never considered complete (sorry, guys). Everything we do should be revisited periodically to make sure it is still valid. Before entering the campaign phase, the persona should be evaluated and tested against any new data. Are there any changes? Are there new personas that need to be created? Is the new campaign aligned with this persona? Are they adopting new or different media? Technology? Interests? Habits? This work is often overlooked, but it will make the difference between the success and failure of a campaign.

Personas should be nurtured like we do with real relationships to keep them fresh. Often, brands that are partnered with an agency for a long time (it does still happen sometimes, trust me) the strategy team notices a sudden shift in audience. The truth is, the shift is almost never sudden. The persona and audience has evolved over time and just wasn't being measured. Good campaigns reach the core audience - your persona - but also expand the audience by bringing in new people with ~~tangential~~ related interests.

Takeaway: What makes a good persona? Critical thinking, but not overthinking. Notice that none of the data points listed above are unusual or hard to find. It is a combination of looking at data, determining what is valuable and discarding the rest. Step one: gather. Step two: edit. What makes a bad persona? A data sheet. A persona's value is in the belief it creates of an actual person living in the world. People will create ideas and experiences for people, not for demographics or cartoons.

CUSTOMER JOURNEY

You have probably noticed some trends in the book so far. Many of the tools and tactics I have described are not static. They move. They change. They evolve. Change cannot be stopped, so we had better find ways to harness it for our advantage. You will not be surprised then, to see that our concept of a customer journey is also a living initiative.

A customer journey map should not be viewed as a deliverable. It is a tool the agency and client create together. I find that an experience map is best if you don't know exactly where the problem is. Glitches in brand experiences are often found where users cross or combine channels. Especially in larger companies, there is an owner for each channel but sometimes not the same person or organization. As a result, organizations need a single view of the experiences they create for their customers or prospects. This is where a map comes in very handy.

An outside perspective of the customer experience is ~~invaluable~~ necessary because it is difficult for insiders to remain objective. As we discussed in Chapter 5, people have a tendency to rationalize. We do this when projects fail or underachieve by finding ways to explain away the poor performance as a fluke. "Well, Kyle was out sick that week." "The project management organization dragged their feet on documentation." An effective customer journey map requires honesty. It has to tell the truth about experience from the customer point of view, no excuses.

Technology and changes in customer expectations are putting more emphasis on the integration of channels and touchpoints that support customers who are attempting to satisfy their goals and needs. Smart organizations have realized a lack of integration is a major competitive risk, or ripe for disruption. Where consumers feel, or even sense friction, between touch points they begin looking for other options. This is how your clients lose customers every day.

If a customer cuts a coupon off of a print FSI and brings it to a restaurant, it is scanned and accepted. The customer is happy. If that same customer clicks a link on Facebook for a coupon from a franchisee and the coupon isn't accepted at their nearest store, they don't take the complexity in stride. They are frustrated. They may not be back.

Let's start our discussion about journey maps with the end in mind. The biggest difference we see in our model for customer journey mapping is that it is designed to be altered for the better. Customer journey maps clients have shared with us are presented as documents frozen in amber. This is troublesome to me because it suggests the customer, company and market don't change. They do. All of them do. When presented as a static document it makes the brand a prisoner of the customer journey and not empowered to fix it.

Knowledge maps should not be created without an action attached. The desired outcome of a customer journey map is to identify one major area to be improved and a plan for doing so.

Our view of the customer journey also is rather cynical. We map from the perspective of the consumer's intentions and not from the client's media plan.

Did you notice I haven't mentioned the traditional marketing funnel in this book? It no longer exists for most brands. Awareness; Interest; Consideration; Intent; Evaluation; Purchase. This was valid once. The internet has rendered this idea impractical in many cases.

People can–and more frequently do–start with intent. They may remember a problem they want to solve suddenly and go to the web to find the answer. Maybe they want to find a vitamin supplement for their aging pet. They Google it and end up on Amazon. In this case, they experience intent before awareness because they are working from goals they wish to accomplish. They are not seeking a new brand to buy. They evaluate and purchase within 15 minutes.

Or someone may be reading an article about bicycling they found on Facebook. They had no awareness of a new seat innovation when they began reading the article. They click directly to a comparison site to read reviews and buy a different seat than the one mentioned in the article. Describe that purchase funnel.

For some reason the customer journey is always mapped with the end benefit coming to the brand. It's just not realistic. The customer journey is the user experience. That's what you're mapping. Each touchpoint, every interaction with the brand is the overall UX for your brand. User experience as a term was born in the digital product world, but the lines between digital and physical world have been erased (but please never say 'phygital').

The original use of the map was to determine how consumers found the product, moved to trial and ~~advanced~~ continue to loyalty. Consider this: most brands today have more owned media channels than there were media formats when the customer journey was first made popular. In a world with limited avenues for discovery, that simple view was great. We can build on this to expand our understanding of all they ways the consumer interacts with the brand and where they can move closer to or further from loyalty.
Once you have identified glitches in the experience, you have the opportunity (or responsibility) to ~~devise~~ invent and recommend improvements. In the original journey maps the answer was *always* an ad campaign because awareness fixed everything then. There is so much more we can do today to relate the brand and customer across platforms. Agencies are so much better equipped to create experiences that break down friction and create loyalty for our clients.

Julian Cole of BBDO defined touchpoints very well. He points out that touchpoints are not the media channel or ad as referenced above. We agree that is too narrow. He believes the touchpoint is the relationship between the person and the brand. Cole defines a touchpoint as the intersection between a person's specific need in a time and place. That means it might or might not be brand territory. People may think about problems they need solved whether they know the brand exists or not.

A solid customer journey map goes far beyond marketing. It provides a shared frame of reference around the customer experience for the entire company. This will build organizational understanding of those customer behaviors and needs across channels and beyond. This is how companies can improve products, business processes and, yes, even marketing.

The map addresses a more fundamental goal; making it easier to understand what customers want. It will provide new insights about customers and prospects along with reinforcement for known insights. A successful map will make the customer easier to know, and easier to create solutions for. The context of the map brings these to life so insights are easy to understand and act on. This helps push the brand towards the customer first thinking that successful brands ~~employ~~ use.

We use four stages borrowed from the geniuses at Adaptive Path and modified for our own purposes.

1. DISCOVER:

Start with whatever has already been done. If a journey has already been mapped, we start there. If not, we dig into any customer data that we can, including sales and marketing. The goal is to get to know the customer, we get to know the customer very well. We will conduct our own research which might be customer or prospect surveys, focus groups or when necessary, more advanced research to break out implicit motivations.

Keep in mind loyalty is about relationships. We need to have a complete view of the potential positives and negatives of those relationships so we also get to know the people on the front lines, the retail or sales staff. The research listed above might apply here, too. This is a great time to conduct secret shopper and shopalong activities or to observe staff interacting with retailers. During discovery, we interview people across the client organization as well as vendors and partners to better understand processes and context for what the customer sees.

2. MAP:

This is where we ~~assemble~~ put together the touchpoints. We might do this in a group workshop with our client. Pro tip: a lot of people at your clients' companies hate workshops. They find it insulting that the agency believes they can get together for a half-day or day and fix everything. They find it frustrating to give up time they don't have to debrief you. They want the outcome, but they don't want to feel like they're doing your job.

The goal is simple in the map phase: identify each

touchpoint through the eyes of your persona(s). If you are able to conduct new research with customers, you'll have some fresh insights. But if you are drawing on the personas alone, put yourself in their shoes. Imagine what they are thinking at each stage. We sort touchpoints across channels and devices as well as the customer behavior at each point. Then we plot them in a logical order and challenge each one. Is the touchpoint as smooth as it can be *for the customer?* What are their specific needs and emotions in each time and place?

It's also a good idea to map your competitors if possible. Comparing the experiences side by side will reveal opportunities for improvement as well as communication of differentiation.

3. REPORT:

In this phase, we share the learnings which will shape an improved customer experience. This should end up being more than a book report of the experience. To make sure this happens we bring audio, video, photos or verbatims from customers and staff to make each element real. The organization needs to begin hearing what areas might be soft or subject to over-investment. Let's help the client understand where they may have legacy spending that is less important to customers or to the overall journey.

The report we share needs to tell a powerful story to our client that presents a renewed business goal. At the conclusion of that report, we want to leave our clients inspired to act to improve things for their customers.

4. ACT:

This is where the map is turned into a plan. We go deeper to clarify issues and align priorities for the map; some of these have already been raised in the report. Some points will be new items your team will find after refining the map based on feedback and upon further review.

We delve into the items that were highlighted as opportunities or threats in the report and potentially create more detailed maps for key interaction points. We have to understand the nuance at these points. We also begin to look forward to a desired, customer-centric state by adding in potential new touchpoints or improved interactions with reduced friction. As we will go into more detail in Chapter 11, we predict outcomes. If these changes you suggest are made, how will business improve? Provide projections on the metrics they care about; the metrics that drive their bonus. Make it meaningful and valuable. These predictive estimates are the permission companies need to act. Without them, they simply can't.

After reviewing the entire map, recommend one item to fix. Initiatives might seem small when the map is on your laptop screen. Consider that each change might involve dozens of people and multiple departments. Don't try to turn the entire business upside down. Get a hold of yourself. Make a case for the most critical element that needs to be fixed. Once fixed, map the journey again to identify new benefits or challenges caused by the repaired touchpoint.

I've placed the customer journey map in the foundational phase. Ideally you start with a blank slate to gather context and the trust of a new client to shape their business. That's not always how it works. I have observed agency personnel uncomfortable asking an existing client questions about their business for fear of appearing out of touch. "Shouldn't we already know this?"

Before we move on to the second phase of strategy, remember: it is important to ask questions when you do not have the information you need. If that information has already been shared, take the time to find it. Ask internally first, obviously. But if you are being tasked with resetting the brand or developing strategies for a new product or line, get the answers first.

This phase is all about context. Knowing what is happening with the company, customers and with the market is the only way to know what else *could* happen. I've provided tools for understanding the competitive environment, the company and current and potential customers. You won't ever use them all on a single brand. Use the tool that is most appropriate based on the assignment or the business challenge (as you understand it) or the one that will deliver the specific answers you seek.

9. PHASE II: CAMPAIGN

The work you have completed in the foundational phase
sets up the brand brief. If you've completed the 5,000 things
I listed in the last chapter, there is enough detail to have a
thorough understanding of the audience, the competitive
set and potential disruptors along with the brand and the
company behind it. And now you get a campaign
assignment. Though the campaign needs to align with

and reflect the brand, the goals of a given campaign are usually more specific than the overall goals of the business. In this chapter, I will bounce back and forth between the overall brand and the campaign as you will when you write a campaign brief. We can't know what shape a campaign should take until we understand the way customers relate to the brand.

One simple way to do this is the FCB Grid. This device has been around since 1980 when Richard Vaughn developed it at, you guessed it, Foote, Cone & Belding. Knowing where the brand or product lives on this grid helps you understand the direction for your campaign brief. In other words: What can we ask consumers to do?

In Quadrant 1 are products that require a lot of mental processing and involvement to buy and use - these are high consideration products. A laptop or a car are in this area. You need to compare products using your System 2 thinking, looking at benefits and tech specs for example.

Quadrant 2 holds highly involved emotional products. I put diverse categories like jewelry and coffee in this area. Customers spend time with the product but the heart and senses guide preference for products in this quadrant. A ring may have an extra sparkle. Coffee beans may have a richer scent. When senses trigger feeling, emotions take over.

Quadrants 1 and 2 are typically reserved for more expensive items. The beauty of the grid is that items aren't plotted in the dead center of each quadrant. Could a car cross into

FCB GRID

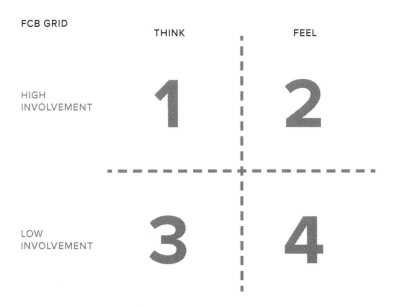

	THINK	FEEL
HIGH INVOLVEMENT	1	2
LOW INVOLVEMENT	3	4

Quadrant 2? Of course. Volvo makes an effort to move there by putting the focus on safety. Once a consumer decides they need to protect their family when driving, it may become an emotional play in Quadrant 2.

Quadrant 3 has our 'low consideration' purchases. Paperclips live in this area along with products that are more commoditized and purchased without much thought. Most of the time these are products that are not highly branded, and we probably don't assess the purchase until we've brought it home and used it.

In the final quadrant are the low involved emotional purchases. I compare these to impulse buys. When you're at the checkout line at your grocery store, there is a reason the candy is lined up with the tabloid magazines. You're bored.

You're tempted. You buy. Quadrant 4 holds the items that we buy to satisfy these simple temptations.

Another tool I use that is similar are continuums for the brand. For example, when working on a digital strategy for a frozen vegetable brand, the client wanted something 'interactive' and flashy. They were citing tech and publishing companies. I showed them these continuums to reframe the product.

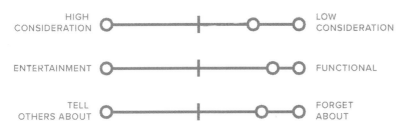

These were continuums I made up for that particular product to make this point: the digital existence of these frozen peas should mirror the experience in the customer's cart, freezer and plate. The product was sitting squarely in Quadrant 3. It's a low involvement product. I might look at the sodium content, compare price to the store brand and then move on. The digital experience should be equally low involvement; something simple like recipes or grocery shopping help and probably not a messaging app with Snapchat integration.

UNIQUE SELLING PROPOSITION VS. BRAND PROMISE
Once, every brand had a unique selling proposition. The USP was the brand's supposed competitive advantage. A beautiful notion from an idyllic time. Though most products do have differences from their rivals, they aren't all differences that are relevant or important to their target consumers.

Instead, the USP became yet another ~~repository~~ dumping ground for jargon or marketing fluff. Look at all the deodorant on the shelf at your pharmacy. There is no meaningful difference that couldn't be copied if a rival cared to. The ingredients are mostly identical or close enough to consumers. Each of those has a USP displayed on the packaging or else buried somewhere in a Powerpoint deck.

If you worked at the company trying to sell deodorant, you would know the ~~intricacies~~ small details that make your product different. When you brief the agency, you would point out those differences and magnify them. And why not? From an internal perspective, those differences are what you and your team worked so hard on to develop this product. Those details would validate you. Or your boss.

But a strategist is also a diplomat. You have to find the information that makes it OK for the client to understand that their chemical compound, though different, is not meaningful to the consumer. Again research can play a role to identify, confirm or debunk a USP. In-home user tests, interviews, focus groups or surveys will help find the reasons why people buy your product or competitors. If you go in open-minded the research can guide you.

What would the USP be for a chocolate bar? It's chocolate, nuts, crisped rice, caramel. There really isn't anything truly 'unique.' Yet, we kept offering them to fill the space in the strategy for a USP. Tradition isn't a bad thing, it's just a waste of time in some cases. The Unique Selling Proposition has value if, and only if, the product actually has one. If not, leave it behind. As with all the tools listed in this book, take what's useful for creating better work and skip what's left. That's why Snickers has success talking about hunger, and not a specific product detail.

It is worth spending time searching for a USP. It is a powerful connection to your target audience. The next best thing is understanding the market your product or brand serves and make sure your brand is the leader in that area. If your client sells furniture, for example, you may need to own 'comfort.' Or you may need to own 'decor.' But your client needs to be perceived as the best in the market of their customer need to be the category leader. Michellin may be known for safety, but if customers didn't ~~associate~~ connect 'safety' with tires, sales would be down the drain and there would be an RFP out.

Some in the industry quip that there are only eight strategies to sell anything. That may actually be an overestimate. Phil Barden lays out the top six motivations that drive consumers and can be the basis for your strategy.

Barden backs this with neuroscience and a diagram of the parts of the brain activated by each motivation in *Decoded*. (Worth reading!) He lists the three primary implicit consumer (and human) goals as *security, autonomy* and *excitement*. He adds the additional goals of *discipline, adventure* and *enjoyment*. His feeling, and I can't disagree, is that this list "is complete in the sense that nothing important is missing when it comes to analyzing the motivational drivers of categories, brands and communications."

Understanding the implicit goals of consumers is why I don't believe in the USP. The USP implies that the additive chosen by a food engineer is more important to purchase than the desire of the customer. It ain't. Usually.

Instead, I subscribe to the commitment a brand will make to the customer to meet their goal; explicit or implicit. Marketers want to build relationships with customers, they want to ~~transcend the transactional and become a trusted resource~~ build loyalty. Customers probably don't want this in all reality. Admit to yourself that you don't want to be friends with your jeans, you just want to wear them. But if you want to help your client build a brand that is attempting to be meaningful to customers, then you will want to write a brand promise.

The brand promise is quite literally the promise the brand can make to its best customers - and keep. Your job in strategy is to build on a foundation of truth. But here's how this idea differs from the USP. The promise has to meet the customer at least half way. Michelin tires promise to be the safest tires for your car. That's a promise the customer cares about, based on implicit goals. In this case: security. A USP for tires might be the combination of reinforcement mesh and tread pattern providing advanced grip. Most consumers don't care. They care about being safe on the road. When they're researching tires, they *might* read *how* the tires provide that safety, but in all likelihood they will look at price and read reviews. If anything.

"And keep." If those last two words won't hold true in any draft of the brand promise, throw out the idea. The promise itself has to be true too of course, but if it can't be virtually guaranteed, that's not the promise you want the brand to make. So it's all about ~~validating~~ proving the promise. This can be the first stage of a campaign brief. This is why I rarely use service in any form as a brand promise. It's too easy to fail - too many variables, too hard a promise to keep.

Michelin could simply demonstrate the stopping power of their tires with videos or even print ads to show how much farther other tires slid. It's a powerful way to prove the promise.

The campaign phase is all about building the triangle that connects the brand, the customer and their goals. The three things must all align to earn a sale or to build loyalty. We use campaigns to demonstrate that the brand understands the customer and their goals. Often we talk about the emotional response of consumers to our advertising. While emotion is important, it's more important for the advertising or message to get consumers to feel they will be able to achieve their goals.

The brand promise is the communication of the explicit goals of the customer. *This brand will let you do this.* The campaign needs to be designed to touch the implicit goals Barden gave us above. The brand promise identifies the 'what,' the campaign presents the 'how.' If there's an emotion to be pulled from the consumer, it might be "you get me and what I'm trying to do."

10. CREATIVE BRIEFS

Of course, the campaign begins with the creative brief. There are a dozen names for this document and hundreds of formats. The information relevant to the creative team for a social campaign brief is different than the information needed for a TV campaign. I've been collecting and comparing briefs from agencies around the world to see if there are any major breakthroughs out there in the wild. Jargon break: I use the term 'creative team' here. Please know the team might include a copywriter and art director of any level, along with people from content, social, development, media, and public relations departments, and beyond. I've chosen to summarize to the traditional term for simplicity.

As part of the request I made to strategists at each shop, I promised I wouldn't publish their brief. I find it interesting so many agencies and strategists protect their brief like intellectual property. I had never thought of our brief that way and have shared it often. We tinker with ours regularly, always trying to improve it. When we see a better idea, we use it. I'm going to share the current brief with you below (which writing this book has lead me to), along with the reasons why each section is included.

The base pieces of the document were adapted from a single-page version of the Richards Group brief we found online. But we've been adding and amending over time, always striving to keep the template to one page. I believe a brief should be brief. I've never seen one that's too short. I have worked at agencies with a double sided 11"x17" brief. Though chock full of information, and written by extremely smart planners and account executives, the document was just too cumbersome.

As a former creative director, I'm comfortable admitting we used the brief as a crutch as well as an excuse. Keep the thing short. Be decisive about what information goes in and what gets cut. Art directors and copywriters are great at keying in on single words or short phrases and building whole worlds out of them. If you are doing your job as a strategist, you know which phrases you want them to key in on. Give them fewer paths, ideally one, to travel.

We do add a second page for specs and mandatories which we try to separate from the brief itself.

S Λ N T Y   CREATIVE BRIEF

Client: Date: Job #:

Media Mix: Internal: To Client:

Why are we advertising?

Whom are we talking to?

What goal will we help them to accomplish?

What is the prevailing category convention?

What do they currently think?

What would we like them to think?

What is the single most important idea our audience must accept?

Why should they believe it?

What is the personality we will convey?

What are campaign, media or copy mandatories?

santy.com

Well, there it is in all its glory. Yay. Before going through each section, let's talk about the kind of information that is best for completing the brief. If you think about writing a brief as filling out a form, I'm sorry but you should close this book. You have wasted your time. For the rest of you, the goal is to pack this document with relevant insights.

What isn't an insight? An insight is not a statistic. An insight is often based on statistics. An insight is not anecdotal observation. Anecdotal observations may be the basis for research that informs an insight. An insight is an example that gives people focused understanding of the problem they are being asked to solve. A good insight is true (table stakes). What you are aiming for is a great insight which is true and gets the creative team running full speed towards a solution. Insights are the fuel for the creative team.

I recently presented a brief to our Chief Creative Officer Ken Spera. He's usually very thoughtful and patient when hearing a brief, asking questions and probing but not overly excited. After reading through this particular brief though, he said "This is an example of a fantastic brief." Ever the researcher, instead of self high-fiving, I asked "Have other briefs been bad?"

"No," he said. "This one is just written in a way that gives me the information and also gets me excited to work on this assignment. I can't wait to get started with this!"

That's the job. Inform and inspire. We usually include some examples of great work in the category or campaigns along similar strategic territory when we download the creative teams. But this is an important point to get into before we go through the segments of the brief and their intent. This may seem overly simple but: Words matter. Especially on a brief.

Choose carefully. Edit wisely. Spend time on every word. The goal is the reaction Ken gave the brief, which I hadn't even intended. He circled the exact words I was focused on when I drafted the brief. He was moving down the path I had plotted and he was excited to do so.

Think about the briefings you hold. How often is there a debate over phrases or even over single words. Clients want different descriptors of their product. They want words from their internal Powerpoint. The creatives want more action words. Somebody demands that you add the word 'authentic' (don't). There is nuance to language and it shapes ideas early. There's a difference between 'fast' and 'quick' which will matter a lot to someone who is about to spend two weeks thinking about this brief. Embrace the debate. Share your brief and don't feel that it's final. Certainly have a point of view, and come with a crafted document you are proud of, but don't lock in and prevent improvements.

The components of the brief we use at Santy are shown above. I'll add description of why it is included and the information I am seeking for each section. Remember, even completed, the goal is to keep the brief to a single page, which is not always possible. I have written drafts that were initially five pages but then edited to a little more than one.

While shorter is better, it has to be complete and impactful. For example, the brief I wrote for the book cover and initial art for Under Think It went onto a second page with all the publisher specs and mandatories. But all the important information is on the first page.

After an overview of the brief format, I will create a sample brief to help bring it to life. For the book, let's write a fictional brief for **Hotel Tonight**, a brand I've never worked on and have no relationship to. If the brief format seems self explanatory, you can jump ahead to the sample which follows:

Why are we advertising?
This is as straightforward as it seems. We do sometimes change the verb 'advertising' to something more specific based on the project. For reasons I don't understand, we overthink this on many, many briefs. As stated earlier, the first question is "What is the real problem we are trying to solve?" Sometimes the answer is simply to increase sales of product X. Sometimes it is to convince the buyer at Costco to choose brand Y. Sometimes to increase NPS scores. Get to the root goal the advertising is being asked to solve.

To whom are we talking?
This is your target audience. Don't reinvent the wheel. Use your persona data, if you have it. If not, build on what the client gives you using the tools in the persona section. Dig into the geographic area or social listening to bring relevant information forward. Pull the most critical information about the persona or target for the assignment, which aligns

with achieving the goal identified in the previous question.

It is always better to organize a brief around a tribe. What specific groups of people are we appealing to and what do they have in common as it relates to the product? The more you can clarify this, the tighter your brief will be. We are never talking to everyone. And we're rarely talking to all of a sub-group either. Figure out who will be most receptive and why.

What goal will we help them to accomplish?
If the product is not of use, the customer will not use it. Understand the goal the customer has that your client's brand or product solves. This might be category level or something more specific. A brand like Burger Lounge may claim "our restaurant provides the only grass fed beef burgers" but something like "we provide nutritionally superior fast food" is more aligned with a consumer's goals. Most people want to eat better but few are super specific about grass-fed beef hamburgers. For Kleenex, they stay at a category level. The goal consumers can partner with Kleenex to achieve is a clean and comfortable nose.

Be honest with yourself. Think about what goals the audience really has, and what business your client is really in. If you don't buy it, neither will your creative team.

This goal also should guide the emotion and tone of the communication. Is the goal something light like the Burger Lounge example above? Or something serious like home security?

What is the prevailing category convention?
Go read Zag by Marty Neumeier. Putting in writing how the category is currently communicated and sold is key to creating a message that has any hope of standing out. Try to distill this down to a single line by the key or dominant players. In complex markets, there may be no single prevailing message convention. Tesla, for example, could cite a dozen message modes from car companies. Instead, they had a strategy early on to compete with luxury cars like Mercedes-Benz and BMW. They focus on those messages and create experiences to disrupt them.

These next three sections work in concert together to build the heart of the brief. Obviously, the entire brief needs to be cohesive, but these three sections are intimately connected. When we write a brief we talk about what the audience thinks and what we want them to think can lead to what is possible for us to persuade them to believe.

What do they currently think?
Now that we have identified the group or groups we hope to influence, we need to know where they stand. Of course, they think a lot of things. The purpose of the brief is to paint a picture of the situation. We can rule out a few topics. Let's restrict this to what they think about the goal they have, the brand or the category.

This, along with the category convention section, is used to depict the current status in the category. If we're talking about an acquisition or conquest-style campaign, then we are describing the state of mind of the customers of our competitors. I recommend highlighting the way this person views weaknesses our client's brand addresses. What makes the goal they are solving harder or less satisfying when using the competitor?

Most ads reach existing customers, intentionally or unintentionally. When writing a brief for our current audience, we would probably address the way the target views our client's own weaknesses or a strength of competitors.

In either case, regardless of who the audience is, the responses to this and the next section are written as quotes as if they are pulled directly from research respondents. If you're drawing from focus groups, customer feedback or survey research, feel free to use ~~verbatims~~ quotes. One or two sentences will do the trick followed by a short one-sentence description when additional context it required.

I also encourage writing them in common English, not fancy business speak. Use contractions, incorrect grammar and slang to make it feel real. As you've seen throughout the book (starting with the title) I believe formality can hold us back. In this case added words or formality often keeps the brief from landing with the creatives. If you're writing a brief for a private jet service, the quote may be more formal as that's how the audience speaks. I don't write them strictly from the voice of the target customer, I write them to connect the mindset of the target customer with the creative team.

What would we like them to think?

After they see our campaign, what would be the best thing the target could think? Obviously there's no value in responses like "I should give brand x a try" or "Gee, sounds like brand x will help me accomplish goal y." Dig deep. How has their perception changed in a perfect world that will allow them to see your point, and be willing to move along the customer journey?

Again, this section is written in the form of a quote from your target audience. It can be an actual verbatim or a fictional quote representative of the audience. And this, too, might be something you have observed from an actual customer who's had a revelation about the brand.

What is the single most important idea our audience must accept?

This is the critical segment of the brief. The creative team needs to register this idea and bring it to life. Write it in a way they will understand and be inspired. It has to rev them up. In most books on creative briefs, they say a tight brief can't be faulted for bad work. Be specific. Be bold. Be clear.

Read Luke Sullivan's *Hey Whipple, Squeeze This*. It's an amazing look at the creative process from a master of the craft. He discusses why beating this point up is critical. He subscribes to the idea that it needs to be an extremely focused point. And others have pushed this notion further. Watching some talks by Pete Favat and Matt O'Rourke from Deutsch, they've discussed the idea this portion of the brief is the campaign. According to the pair, the answer written by the planner should be the campaign idea and the creative team is assigned to give it a compelling skin. They believe the strategy is the solution.

Most briefs come down to the goals listed above (or variations of those) and one other element. Offense or defense. Let's remember for a moment that this is commerce. We are trying to sell and consumers are buying. Some purchases are best classified as offense (as in sports) - people are looking to acquire, to possess, to own. They are motivated to buy. This is a powerful notion behind luxury goods. Offense is more associated with non-necessities.

Then there is defense. People hate losing things. Hate it. For necessities and commodities, a common brief is promising - buy this so you don't lose that. Insurance, for example. Education. Diet or light foods. When crafting your single idea, think about whether their goal qualifies as offense or defense. The single idea should complement their perception of that goal.

Why should they believe it?
This is the section for all the facts you have about the product that lead you to the single most important idea. These reasons to believe can be a combination of stats and facts. Make sure they are true. Don't ask the creative team to build a case based on bullshit. When presenting creative, they will cite these reasons as support for their ideas. Know before you brief them whether you'll be comfortable with it or not.

These facts often become the foundation for copy or support

graphics for the campaign. You have to really dig to put the strongest argument forward. Your client will supply you with several points as starters. Again, you are trying to connect the brand with consumers' goals, so this isn't a time for regurgitating or copy/pasting. Choose the most relevant and compelling points. Spend time thinking about each to discover if there's another way to look at it that may add meaning. There is no worse feeling as a strategist than presenting a brief to the creative team nobody believes in.

What is the personality we will convey?
This final section should be summarized as succinctly as possible. If you're listing adjectives, keep it to three or less. Warm, cheerful, optimistic. Pragmatic, technical, expert. If there is a show or celebrity that matches your vision, include them and links to specific clips to help bring it to life.

Personality is important because you are shaping the voice of the campaign. Up top you've set up the goals of the consumer, then the main idea. Here you're setting up the way the consumer wants to be related to. Is the brand a partner? An authority? A friend? A conspirator? You need to decide and have a rationale for why.

SAMPLE BRIEF - HOTEL TONIGHT

Enough theory. Sometimes it takes an exercise to bring it to life. Now for that sample brief for Hotel Tonight. If you're not familiar with Hotel Tonight, the service finds users last-minute deals on hotel rooms. Users of the website or app can book a room on the same day at a deep discount by filling unbooked room inventory. The company doesn't brand itself as a discounter, instead it presents the brand as an opportunity provider. Having done only light research using Alexa.com and Netbase, I'm going to make assumptions about the audience makeup to help complete the brief.

Why are we advertising?
While bookings are important, we need to increase app downloads by 10% to build loyalty behaviors with consumers and sell-in with hotel chains and resellers.

To whom are we talking? (Some big guesses, but go with it)
Ages: 24-54, gender ~neutral, race matches census
HHI $25k-$150k; College educated
A majority of visitors to the website are browsing from work.
Frequent travelers (5-15 trips per year business/personal travel combined)
Interests: travel, airlines, adventurous eaters - avoid chains
Members of multiple loyalty clubs for airlines and hotel, but not highly loyal. Opportunistic about earning points and rewards.
They want the flexibility to efficiently book last minute business trips without paying a premium.

The bold bullet is what we need to decide on. It turns out the the percentage of visitors to Hotel Tonight platforms is more than twice the internet average for people coming from work. A number this high is usually not a coincidence. From this we might infer people are using the site to book business travel. If we can build habit with this group of frequent travelers, we will likely capture their leisure travel as well. We have to decide if this is a business or leisure audience.

To confirm, I conducted a cursory social listening exercise using Netbase to learn more about the context of brand mentions. This is a complicated task as the phrase 'hotel tonight' is used often, organically and not relating to the brand. Looking back one year from today, I was able to narrow down ~100,000 mentions about the brand. Gender and race were confirmed, both match normal averages aligned with the census.

If professionals or entrepreneurs were using the site to book business travel, I would expect a different set of phrases than what was found. Most people are talking about leisure or personal travel, or at least not mentioning the business side of their trips. In addition, business mentions would likely happen during business hours or at least Monday - early Friday. But a look at the common day and time of mentions shows the comments are higher on the weekend, indicating personal travel. This is especially true of '#hoteltonight,' which spikes on the weekend. We'll be targeting opportunistic leisure travelers.

These #hoteltonight posts also are informative for the brief. People are calling out the city or the event they are attending, but rarely calling out the hotel. They're not concerned much about the brand or status of the hotel though some do praise the place the app enabled them to book. They're celebrating experiencing these trips and events. On Monday, they will have stories to tell and Hotel Tonight will be part of them.

What goal will we help them to accomplish?
Hotel Tonight allows people to feel the adventure of travel and live more life.

From Phil Barden's list above, Hotel Tonight's offering aligns with security (by promising that a last-minute room is always a click away) and autonomy (by allowing people the freedom to travel at the last minute). The service also aligns with adventure (by promoting the idea you can leave any time without a plan).

What is the prevailing category convention?
Discount hotel chains (think La Quinta, Best Western) sell value through promoting the number of locations and light amenities, such as free breakfast and wifi (really?). Online travel agents (OTAs) and hotel discounters (Hotels.com, Trivago) sell the lowest price and no promises, but require some lead time to get the biggest savings. The biggest rival here is probably Airbnb, whose focus is on experiencing local culture by renting real homes.

What do they currently think?
"I miss out on spontaneous opportunities because it's expensive and hard to find hotels at the last minute." These travelers value spur-of-the-moment experiences and look for ways to maximize the rush. Even OTAs require effort and time with planning and complex comparison.

What would we like them to think?
"If I knew I'd be able to afford a room no matter where I end up, I could go anywhere!"

What is the single-most important idea our audience must accept?
Hotel Tonight takes the pain out of last-minute trips. (Defense)
Hotel Tonight makes great travel stories possible. (Offense)

Overall, the goal of the consumer is an offensive goal. They want to travel to advance in business. The autonomy and adventure of making a late plan to go makes them feel bold and worldly. In this context, even security isn't about loss, but about ensuring they will be able to go and land a room without much trouble. The second option is more in line with the goal and more appropriate.

Why should they believe it?
The app has been downloaded 15 million times. The Hotel Tonight booking process averages 10 seconds. Compared to the lowest published hotel rates, Hotel Tonight's discount averages 17%. Travel booking via mobile devices grew 25% from 2012 to 2015 (Hotel Tonight is mobile only). More than 60% of domestic hotel bookings are made within seven days of arrival, according to Sojern.

What is the personality we will convey?
Confident, savvy, bright.

11. ROLE OF MEDIA

A strong brief is just one component of a successful campaign. As a strategist, it's critical to have a point of view on how you'll deliver the message. To effectively reach the audience, the resulting work has to earn their attention. Read Faris Yakob's *Paid Attention* for a deep look into the complexity of capturing audiences today.

People don't read ads, they read things that interest them and sometimes it's an ad. This is as true now as when Howard Gossage said it. Except today, they have 100 times the amount of potential items to read instead of your ad as they did when he said it. In fact, when it comes to media, your competition isn't just your category rivals. Your competition is every other thing fighting for the attention of your target audience.

Let's say you are selling razors. You're vying for that coveted 18-34 year-old male audience, so you're obviously competing with Gillette, Schick, Barbasol and Dollar Shave Club. Of course. But you're also competing with ESPN, Barstool Sports, Netflix, Fox News, Instagram, Pandora, Cartoon Network, XBOX and Pornhub.

Given the choices I listed, which make up a tiny fraction of the possible options your audience has at any given moment, why on earth would they choose to hear from your brand? So often we are handed an assignment from a client and just start running. "We want to do a social campaign" sounds just like the starting gun for the 100-meter hurdles.

Go back to our core questions again. What is the real problem we are trying to solve? The problem is rarely that the client needs to spend a quarter million dollars on a social media campaign. The problem is ~~more akin to~~ more like improving sales or making the brand relevant with a consumer segment, though there are more specific challenges. This might be a difficult thing to challenge, but it's important to understand why the client is requesting this specific medium. Or to ask if they even understand what they're asking. Dollar Shave Club acquired its sizeable customer base using digital channels, including podcasts before going mass on television and then being acquired. On the other hand, Gillette built its brand on television and won't go away from that medium any time soon, in spite of flagging viewership numbers. One has to wonder, if Gillette launched today would they have found television as useful?

In today's environment, probably not. Television is still the best mass reach vehicle available. If you want to reach a huge audience at once, television is still the best way. U.S. culture is fragmented by interests today, so even the Super Bowl has to compete for attention during its halftime show with counter programming, digital platforms and social media. More people may be cutting the cord every day, but to get a group of likeminded thinkers to see your message at (or around) the same time, TV is your best bet.

Video, like televised ads and content, is the clearest way to tell your brand story or call out your differentiators. How good is it? I recently saw a commercial with my six-year-old son. A few seconds in, he said "Oh, this is a Progressive ad." About five seconds later, a hamster appeared and it was revealed that the ad was clearly not an ad for Progressive (it was for Kia). I turned to him and asked, "Why did you think it was for Progressive?"

"Because it was all white."

I thought for a moment, impressed with my offspring for

obviously being a genius and ignoring the fact that Progressive has branded themselves so well that a six year old recalls their ads, color strategy and presenter. "Do you know what Progressive is?" I asked.

"They sell computers," he said without looking at me.

I'm relieved he didn't understand what insurance is at that age. Most consumers who are old enough to understand can remember Progressive (and Flo) because of how the ads play out on television. They are designed to ~~distinguish~~ separate from their competitors and do so very clearly, using humor. They're designed to be remembered, maybe not for individual spots, but for the brand as a whole. Most brands just don't have the patience to do this as Progressive has for the past decade.

Since people are cutting the cord - or avoiding it altogether - the TV audience has become less mass. It's not that people aren't watching their television, they've just found new ways to get the shows and films they watch.

But they are still spending time with TV, life or time shifted. According to Nielsen's Total Audience Report from Q4 2016, U.S. consumers spent almost 10 times more time watching live TV than the next closest video option - time shifted TV.

They are getting over-the-top and web services like Netflix, Amazon Prime, Hulu and YouTube on their devices, but still using smart TVs and add-ons like Roku or Apple TV to watch. The trick is how to get to some of those audiences because video is powerful regardless of platform. With Netflix ruled out (no ads yet) YouTube is a strong option followed by Hulu which asks consumers to pay to avoid ads (makes you feel good about your line of work, no?).

Longer-form video that can be hosted and distributed on digital platforms can be compelling if done right. Brands can use explainers or story telling to reduce complex products or services or tell their founder's story. YouTube is a great place for this because of the lack of constraints on video length, advanced targeting and audience scale. There are just a ton of people there watching. But be aware, we think about video content as advertising. In reality, when you create a longform video for a CPG company, for example, you are not creating an ad. You are creating a product. A product that competes with content by the video platforms above. And it is now your responsibility to advertise this product and not the CPG itself.

In the digital environment you can promote the longer video using a variety of tools to build anticipation or interest and driving traffic. Small products can launch exclusively on social today - and frequently do. Social media platforms have made it easy for brands to reach their audience very efficiently. I'm skeptical about whether consumers really want to talk to brands on their favorite social channels or if they just want to get coupons and freebies. I've worked on cult brands that seem to draw the attention of the internet and grow like crazy.

I've also puzzled at well postured brands that just can't figure out how to crack social media.

It's not always for lack of trying. Can anyone explain why Denny's and KFC are so successful on social but IHOP and Popeye's aren't? The key comes from understanding how to be useful to consumers in the context of the space. In social, those successful brands have figured out how to provide sharable entertainment. Their products are not always useful, but entertainment is useful pretty often.

I don't believe people want to have a conversation with a brand. Not a real conversation. They want to shop the brand when they have a goal. They want a coupon that will save them money. Now. And they want a place to vent when the server at Red Robin refuses to sing happy birthday to their daughter (I'm not bitter). But Denny's has figured out how to make breakfast food interesting enough that people follow along and treat Denny's as part of the gang on Twitter. I can't say for sure that it improves sales. But people do love the jokes.

Part of social is just being there in a way that reminds people you exist, the same as we did on television. "Oh, right. I haven't had a burger in a while." Even when we get it right, it's hard to know if what we're doing is improving business directly from social. And for some reason, we're all conditioned to track down exactly what moved people to buy. Google refers to it as the zero moment of truth. The attributable moment when the consumer bought in.

We didn't track TV that way, because we couldn't. We could only correlate except in DRTV environments. Even now, as new targeted television is possible via addressable TV, tracking it isn't easy. The promise of digital, and now social, was that we can track every click. Unfortunately there are not very many of them to track.

People hate ads. People hate bad ads more. Banners are almost always bad ads. The worst. So people especially hate them and avoid clicking them. You have accidentally tapped more banners than you have intentionally clicked in your life.

Well, we thought web banners were the worst. Until we saw them on mobile. Now we know what hate is. Banners on mobile are so detested that Apple went from launching iAds in 2010 to adding an ad blocker to it's own operating system and browser by default. Because Apple knows a thing or two about experience and knows that serving people the very worst form of advertising when they're trying to read four point text on their device is suboptimal shitty.

What is optimal on mobile? I'm not sure mobile is a medium, though it's referred to as one and separated in media plans and keynote speeches. Mobile should be translated to: the most relevant thing at virtually all times. I watch videos on my phone. I read Twitter (way too much) on my phone. I check in to bars on my phone. If I have a question about an old TV show, I look it up on my phone.

That is the disconnection between the mass audience of TV and action. TV is what is on. But even while you're watching TV, you can be playing on your phone. Your TV is eight feet from your couch, but the phone is only 14 inches from your face. And when do you interact with brands on your phone? Only on your own terms, the same way you do everything else on your phone. Gossage was right. We were trained on dumb phones that whatever the phone shows us is most urgent. Then it stuffed all the knowledge and entertainment of the entire world into that glass rectangle.

Brands look pretty good on Instagram, posing as your friends just to get in front of you for 1,080 pixels. Is that short camouflaged image building brand equity? I don't believe a single exposure on any medium can convey the brand in a meaningful way. So, the question is how long does a consumer need to follow your brand on Instagram and how many posts do they have to see in their feed to get the brand idea across?

I don't have the answer. I know this: Facebook, well-conceived Twitter ads and retargeted mobile banners are effective at driving conversions. In other words, you can get a person to click or even buy your product using those media. But are you building the brand? Is anyone even seeing your posts on Facebook?

Snapchat is showing the cracks that are caused when brands joining the platform have to try so hard to not be advertising, they don't get any advertising-like results. Brands have to play hard to get, and consumers don't come chasing them there. They're looking for entertainment when they open Snapchat, and aren't as receptive to educational or even informational content. This means Instagram may be the best of the bunch for social media and branding.

Their focus on visual communication is fantastic for brand building and the additions of multiple formats for video and continuing storytelling help the brand exist as a narrative; always moving forward. Never quite the same as the day before. Doing things. Going places. Just like your friends.

Except brands are not your friends. Social media was built on relationships between people. Not really between people and companies. Like a popular bar or coffee shop, people go when there are other people inside. They don't go to the bar to see an ad, no matter how relevant or creative it might be. They log onto Facebook to see what friends and family are up to. They log on to LinkedIn to see what colleagues are doing. They may see an ad they respond to, but that's not the ~~raison d'etre~~ reason it exists. People don't want to be friends with brands. Even influencers, the living embodiment of media are not your friends. In fact, we're seeing a trend towards micro-influencers because consumers don't relate to those influencers who have hustled enough to build followings enough to attract ad dollars. The irony. Brands try to move down the media chain as influencers become too big to partner with.

As you've probably considered, there's a big gap in media spectrum. Television seems like a big investment but a bit of a risk, given the way consumers viewing habits are changing. Social is fantastic on a tactical level, but it delivers far less in terms of brand building. Bob Hoffman pointed out an article from *Harvard Business Review* highlighting experiments by Leslie John, Oliver Emrich, Michael Norton and Sunil Gupta (https://hbr.org/2017/03/whats-the-value-of-a-like). They tested purchase intent amongst a group of Facebook followers of a new cosmetics brand and non-followers. Whether they liked the brand on Facebook or not, they were equally likely to purchase. "Across 16 studies, we found no evidence that following a brand on social media changes people's purchasing behavior," the authors state.

You might be shaking your head at this point and thinking I'm a Luddite. Afterall, I'm not even on Facebook, Instagram or Snapchat (anymore). Hear me out first. Why do we feel the need to measure every aspect of every platform and try to compare them head to head? We accept that television isn't measurable (yet). We accept that radio has no accountability. But since social is born from digital, and there are buttons near it, then we must track clicks. Thus, I can say with confidence (arrogance?) that social makes a great transactional media.

Radio is known as the promotional medium. Airing spots or partnering with stations through events like remotes (~~prototypical~~ early influencer marketing) is believed to drive traffic to retail locations. But no one tracks clicks. There aren't many metrics. Until we start talking about streaming radio. Suddenly, when Pandora or Spotify appear in the media deck, the client starts asking about CTR and paying keen attention to new accompanying visual ad units (don't tell anyone, these are 'banner ads.') Is it possible that the clicks here are just gravy? If you believe in the audio medium, then the association of your client's brand with music or content you like - served at a meaningful frequency is the goal. We both know, nobody is clicking a banner ad on Spotify. But I listen to it for hours every day, and rarely hear FM radio. And since I listen to Spotify at my desk and not in my car, is the audio medium still as effectively promotional?

And television - the medium - gets a bad rap, but rarely do people point out the work is out of touch. If you've watched television recently, you have seen a TV ad that showed people on a subway car. Why? One tenth of the country lives reasonably close to a subway. If we're comparing media, and social is all about interests, and mobile is all about proximity - why is TV creative given a pass? Because the creative came from New York and the writer commutes on the subway? Most of your customers don't. If we want television to work for our clients we have to fight to make the work meaningful to our audience. To take it even further, a lot of people working on social content and campaigns are putting real thought into how to create something audiences will relate to, something rich, compact but sprawling stories. Meanwhile, TV ads clumsily mimic iOS swiping functionality or Snapchat effects to seem current - but miss out on what makes them effective. Scale. They can work because they are *not* confined to the new small screen. They can be cinematic.

We like to think that outdoor works together with radio to replicate the effects of television. People exposed to both outdoor and radio for a brand incorrectly 'recall' seeing television ads for that brand. They make the leap likely because they get the audio and potentially a story in the radio format and link it with the visual from the outdoor board. This tells me people are subconsciously imaginative. I don't believe consumers are daydreaming about my clients' brands. Or yours. They fill in the blanks we give them in media and campaigns on their own. Or else, they go to Google after a few impressions and fill in the blanks from there.

Finally, there is poor, poor print. The forgotten child. When I travel to cities with newsstands I marvel that magazines are still being printed and sold. At this point, I expect to see any print being handed out for free like an in-flight magazine. Sometimes, I pick up a magazine in a waiting room and I really enjoy leafing through it. I like print as a foil to the metal and glass of digital. I appreciate a vacation from load times and pop-ups. Even when I'm really enjoying an article, a push notification on my phone pulls me right back, and the magazine is back on the table. Print has become a reinforcement medium for brands big or lucky enough to be able to afford it.

Print lacks the ability to target as specifically as digital. But that raises a point. For a while, this was considered waste. Reaching people beyond your known target. Waste is bad, especially when you're paying for every impression. We've been conditioned to do the conversion math that takes us from the viewing audience to the sale. But it's hard to grow if you are only selling to people who already know the brand. Mass media provides an opportunity to reach people beyond your core customers and look-alikes. When done intelligently that's a good thing.

Your client didn't hire you to guess. They have a business goal and your work is meant to accomplish it. Media has to strike a balance between the goals of the brand and the goal of the consumers. It has to earn awareness while driving conversions, whatever those may be. As you think about the media mix for your campaign, think about what each medium can contribute and how they will work together.

12. PHASE III: POST CAMPAIGN

You've done all the foundational work. You've written a killer brief. You've inspired your team to create an amazing campaign. Insights abound. The media mix is spot on. Now for the big question. Did it work?

Measurement can be one of the biggest challenges. Not because numbers are hard to come by. They aren't. Metrics are everywhere. Your job is to know which ones matter, because most are meaningless on their own. Together, a well-considered set of metrics provides the context to evaluate a campaign and set the table for future work. Without focus, it's just data.

Analytics has become synonymous with insight. It can be, if it's actually been analyzed. Too often, the numbers sit in a dashboard and get forwarded from person to person. Each field is taken at face value as if it means anything. We think some numbers speak for themselves. As I've said earlier, they don't. Some of us refer to bottom-line numbers like sales or traffic, for instance, as single indicators of success. There's probably no explanation necessary behind either of those, right? If sales were good, it was the campaign. Not the offer. Or the media. Or a lucky coincidence a pop star was seen wearing the item. Simple and self-explanatory. If only!

As we just reviewed, campaigns are complex. There are dozens of forces at play in media alone, nevermind all we reviewed about how consumers make choices. Here is a method for knowing how well your campaign worked.

In the early 2000's, Crispin Porter was rumored to have required creative teams to present concepts internally in the form of the press release that would be issued when the work went live. They started with the end in mind and painted a picture of success in the form of press coverage. This gave those who were reviewing concepts a sense of the scale of the idea, as well as the possibility of coverage and potential earned impressions.

We too can start with the end in mind. In our case, we'll imagine a case study for the upcoming campaign. As we are planning the media and writing all the executional briefs for the campaign, we will begin seeing the shape of the campaign. The case study is a great way to begin projecting the measure of success for the client by mapping all the assets to a successful conclusion. Don't get fancy. Follow the familiar case study format.

Our client, "X Co" wanted to "Y." They turned to "Your Agency" to create "Z." Here is a list of tremendous things that resulted.

Have you ever noticed how great case studies skip the mundane crap we find in campaign dashboards? Ever wondered why? Because those numbers are not important. Television points purchased or delivered aren't important unless the goal of your campaign is simple media efficiency. Some of the key questions a winning case study answers involves bottom-line numbers like sales or traffic. What revenue can be attributed from sales tied to your campaign? If you're tracking that, you'll be able to calculate return on investment.

There's no campaign today that will be without a digital center. We're sending people to a landing page, a campaign microsite, an app or a (yuck!) Facebook page. If we're planning for the case study, we'll work with the developers to make sure the site is built to capture the metrics that matter and share them in a way we can use.

Here's an example in which I failed to do this. We worked on a campaign with a client to create an interactive video campaign. Users were sent to the site from social, digital, radio and of course online video. Each user could personalize the video and share it with their friends. Our developers built the site from scratch, so it was flawless. Clean code, customized for our campaign. We added multiple analytics tools so our digital team could review daily and tweak media sources. We built events in that allowed us to quickly track key metrics and critical points in the experience.

We had set KPIs for videos created, videos shared and media metrics. There was a post-campaign coupon that was served to participants that acted as a proxy for purchase. Traffic for the promoted event topped the previous year as did sales. By all counts the campaign was a success. As we reviewed the campaign results I thought about the metrics. We had media results. We had video results. Suddenly the question popped into my mind I wish had arrived six weeks earlier.

The videos we were asking our users to create and share were also media. But I failed to think of that sooner. So the videos weren't properly coded as individual media sources. Each video was an individual referrer from which could have been tracked impressions, completed views, clicks, coupons and additional video creation. This would have proved the campaign assets reached people outside our media audience demonstrating higher ROI for the video and microsites themselves. Had I thought of that, I also would have thought to include a cookie into the viewer software to retarget users leading up to the promoted event. We could have driven additional sales and even better results. The campaign met its benchmarks, but we failed to capture the expanded measurement that would have set us up for better planning for future campaigns.

Earlier, I said satisfaction is a dumb metric. Preference, loyalty, and recommendation are all more meaningful. All the metrics we can easily capture are top line metrics. On their own, they're cheap. Impressions for example, as a media metric. That's the inventory you bought. You could likely predict that before the campaign ran, by taking 90% of the paid media. If we're going to have meaningful metrics, we have to get direct with our counterparts and find out how they measure the campaign on their end. Then figure out how pieces of the campaign impact that number. What metrics are linked to traffic? Which are connected to sales?

You may have done concept testing before the campaign launched. Especially if there was television involved. Use that opportunity as a chance to create a benchmark that can be tested again after the campaign has run. Qualitative research is largely anecdotal, but a properly constructed pre/post study with focus groups should provide insights about how the audience was moved by the campaign, or not. If you're doing a post-campaign study, know what you're looking for.

 If you're launching a new brand, you would need to understand brand awareness and a ranking of the most preferred brands in the category before your campaign. This can be done in groups, but more effectively in a survey. In this case, the quantitative result provides a clear answer on the campaign effectiveness. You can then revisit the results after the campaign to see how you've improved. Has unaided awareness improved? Has anyone begun listing your brand among those with top preference?

Lower awareness for a brand means a different type of campaign, doesn't it? The campaign has to be memorable and present a counterpoint to established brands to carve out a mental position for the brand in the consumer's mind. As aided awareness increases, the campaign has to make the product more valuable to the consumer. That may mean through the literal value proposition of the product, or through elements like humor. The campaign must make the brand sticky to consumers to get them to remember the brand on their own. When a brand achieves unaided awareness, the campaign is about building understanding of the offering and creating preference and loyalty.

AWARENESS > TRIAL > TRAFFIC > SALES > LOYALTY
LOW EMOTION >>>   >>> >>> >>> >>> >>> >>> HIGH EMOTION

Each of these steps is accompanied by consumers' emotional investment. The level of the emotion varies by category, as we discussed earlier. Functional products like staples just don't elicit emotion and likely never will. But brands for products like cars earn a lot of emotion. As we move deeper into awareness and then loyalty, we become more emotionally invested.

And finally, campaigns for brands with established loyalists attempt to build recommendations or improved Net Promoter Score (NPS). Whenever possible, perform a pre-campaign NPS survey. You'll want to understand how the campaign and associated activities changed the recommendation metric. Are people more likely to recommend the brand to a friend post-campaign? When we can't conduct that study, we look at social media sentiment and spontaneous brand mentions. They're not a substitute for NPS or preference studies, but they are less concrete directional indicators.

Like search terms, we can track social mentions of phrases from the campaign. Or the ever-present #hashtag. In the case of search, we can quickly build an understanding on the actions searchers took when they followed their search from the Google box to your campaign microsite. In the case of social, tapping in the tagline might be the end game, like we used to study with search keywords when we looked at volume as a metric. Add on sentiment and there's a layer that adds some value.

Most metrics that are easily gathered are worth what they cost. They have to be combined to mean something. Counting the number of sessions isn't all that useful. But counting the sessions against media sources or earned media starts to tell a story. If it's your job to sell the strategy, it's going to be you that has to explain for the success of the strategy. In my fail example above, I didn't have the forethought to plan for earned media exposure and additional conversions resulting from that exposure.

The further down the funnel you can get with measurement towards the business metrics, the more compelling your case will be. Site visits and bounce rate are meaningless to a business. When we're not dealing with an ecommerce campaign that attributes a direct dollar value to each visitor, we have to use lead-gen conversions as a proxy. In the case above it was coupon downloads.

The reality there is that the coupons were a poor proxy for sales. We had no way to know if the coupon was redeemed. Or saved. We couldn't follow users to a physical restaurant location. Make sure you build your campaign with a strong tie to downstream metrics. If you want to help the business, that's what you do. If you want to be taken seriously by the c-suite, that's what you do.

13. CONCLUSION

Sometimes, we try so hard to be smart that we ~~behave~~ act a little stupid. Don't see the forest for the trees. There is no playbook. There is no one way to work. There is only an approach that is focused on finding the answers and identifying which are the essential answers needed to get to a solution to the problem at hand. Strategy today is a bit like American Ninja Warrior. There may be ways we've seen that are effective at overcoming certain obstacles, but inventive competitors always find new ways to get it done.

It's clear by now that there are no limit to the tools and the ideas that are already out there. Or else this book would be four pages long. As I said at the top, very few of the tools discussed here are my invention. If you take nothing else away from this book, take this: no two assignments are alike, and no two solutions are alike. It's not just your job to mix and match tools to find the answers that lead to great work. It is your privilege. Everything is a remix including your next assignment.

It is so easy to get into your own head (or it's easy for me to into mine) and go all theoretical. While I love theory, and I love hearing ideas in a pure form, that is not the job, strictly speaking.

I've spoken with some great ~~practitioners~~ planners and thinkers and I've been inspired by the creativity they use with whatever tools they've got. The most interesting thing about talking to 20 planners is they have at least 20 unique ways to solve the same problem. No two would go about it the same way. Probably if given the same challenge in a year, they would come back with 20 different solutions. Those looking to advance in strategy will have to adapt to change and bring great ideas forward.

Is this book 100% comprehensive. No. My conversations with planners and marketers across the country continue to show me new ways to work. And those chats reinforce the need for more training, and more communication amongst professionals. I've been amazed how generously most people give their time and brains. Sometimes a tweet triggers a thread that leads to a new perspective. An idea. No printed document could capture everything. But we have to start somewhere.

Any tradesman has a toolbox. A lot of the tools exist in their mind - the know-how to use what's in the box and how to improvise. Don't be afraid to experiment with different tools in different ways. As the expression goes 'Don't use your pliers as a hammer, that's what screwdrivers are for.' Find the right tool for the right time. If you're comfortable with something you can usually get more out of it. Make it your own. Be receptive to new ideas and new voices. Every idea sparks another idea. Hopefully I've collected enough sparks to get you to your next great idea.

BIBLIOGRAPHY
(read these books)

Ariely, Dan. *Predictably Irrational* HarperCollins Publishers, 2009

Barden, Phil. *Decoded: The Science Behind Why We Buy* Wiley, 2013

Gossage, Howard; Goodby, Jeff. *The Book of Gossage* Copy Workshop, 2006

John, Leslie K.; Mochon, Daniel; Emrich, Oliver; Schwartz, Janet. *"What's the Value of a Like?"* Harvard Business Review 2017 *https://hbr.org/2017/03/whats-the-value-of-a-like*

Kahneman, Daniel. *Thinking Fast & Slow* Farrar, Straus and Giroux, 2011

Maslow, Abraham H. *Toward a Psychology of Being* Wiley, 1962

McNish, Jacquie; Silcoff, Sean. *Losing the Signal: The Untold Story Behind The Extraordinary Rise and Spectacular Fall of BlackBerry* Flatiron 2015

Neumeier, Marty. *Zag: The Number One Strategy of High-Performance Brands* New Riders, 2006

Porter, Michael. *Competitive Strategy: Techniques for Analyzing Industries and Competitors* Free Press, 1979

Sullivan, Luke. *Hey Whipple! Squeeze This* Wiley, 2016 (5th Printing)

Yakob, Faris. *Paid Attention* Kogan Page, 2015

Yes, the Red Robin story is true

42238503R00084

Made in the USA
San Bernardino, CA
08 July 2019